Myths of the Creation of Chinese

Zhaoyuan Tian · Shuxian Ye · Hang Qian

Myths of the Creation of Chinese

Zhaoyuan Tian
School of Social Development
East China Normal University
Shanghai, China

Shuxian Ye
Center for Study of Literary Anthropology
Shanghai Jiao Tong University
Shanghai, China

Hang Qian
College of Humanities and Communications
Shanghai Normal University
Shanghai, China

Translated By Tian Zhang, Liang Ming, Jasmine Fan, Xuan Zhang, Hannah Wu

ISBN 978-981-15-5927-3 ISBN 978-981-15-5928-0 (eBook)
https://doi.org/10.1007/978-981-15-5928-0

Jointly published with Shanghai Jiao Tong University Press
The print edition is not for sale in China (Mainland). Customers from China (Mainland) please order the print book from: Shanghai Jiao Tong University Press.

© Shanghai Jiao Tong University Press 2020, corrected publication 2020
This work is subject to copyright. All rights are reserved by the Publisher, whether the whole or part of the material is concerned, specifically the rights of translation, reprinting, reuse of illustrations, recitation, broadcasting, reproduction on microfilms or in any other physical way, and transmission or information storage and retrieval, electronic adaptation, computer software, or by similar or dissimilar methodology now known or hereafter developed.
The use of general descriptive names, registered names, trademarks, service marks, etc. in this publication does not imply, even in the absence of a specific statement, that such names are exempt from the relevant protective laws and regulations and therefore free for general use.
The publisher, the authors and the editors are safe to assume that the advice and information in this book are believed to be true and accurate at the date of publication. Neither the publisher nor the authors or the editors give a warranty, express or implied, with respect to the material contained herein or for any errors or omissions that may have been made. The publisher remains neutral with regard to jurisdictional claims in published maps and institutional affiliations.

This Springer imprint is published by the registered company Springer Nature Singapore Pte Ltd.
The registered company address is: 152 Beach Road, #21-01/04 Gateway East, Singapore 189721, Singapore

Preface

During the National Day holiday of 2016, Shanghai Library launched a lecture series called "The Creation Myths of China". Before that, I was entrusted to invite scholars and decide the topics. The series was to consist of six sessions lectured by three speakers. Then Mr. Shuxian Ye, the expert in mythology and Mr. Hang Qian, the expert in social history both joined me; we co-conducted the entire series.

Initiated by the Shanghai Library, publicized and promoted by the local media, we sparked an interest in creation mythology among the public: the lectures were so well received that none of us had expected. Therefore, Shanghai Library decided to put these lectures together into a book. Through the hard work of the forum organizers and the editors of Shanghai Jiao tong University Press, the book is published. What a hard-earned yet rewarding accomplishment!

Being one of the most modernized cities in China, Shanghai seems to have little inheritance of creation myths. Why people here have such a passion for studying and discussing China's creation myths? I would like to say a few words.

Firstly, Shanghai's social and economic development brings the demand for culture. This is the background. Shanghai has become one of the most affluent cities, and its demand for cultural consumption has increased significantly. Citizens won't be satisfied with simply enjoying imported goods but need more "shanghai-made". For example, the Shanghai National Musical Instrument Factory was in bleak operation more than a decade ago, because at that time, learning music equaled to learning the piano and the violin. Traditional Chinese instruments were difficult to sell. In recent years, the demand for national musical instruments such as Pipa and Guzheng (Chinese zither) has been strong. This trend boosted the performance of Shanghai National Musical Instrument Factory and the manufacturing technology of traditional musical instruments was also improved. Economics development brings cultural confidence. Simple and primary cultural products no longer meet the citizen's needs for upgrading cultural consumption. Therefore, the creation myth, as a somewhat unfamiliar and unique form with rich cultural connotation, naturally becomes the chosen form of cultural consumption.

Secondly, Shanghai needs its own cultural identity. Throughout history, what has embarked in Shanghai is not only colonial culture; in fact, there are as long as 6,000 years of civilization accumulated in the reign. As the Zhangze culture, the Fuquanshan culture, the Guangfulin culture, and the Maqiao culture were gradually discovered, people found that Shanghai used to be a splendid sky. Such a small land had breaded such many ancient civilizations; it is truly worth being proud of and makes Shanghai qualify to declare: it is the important birthplace of the dragon culture, and also the region once governed by the Confucius' only southerner disciple Yan Yan (Ziyou). Only a culture rooted in its country can have a strong vitality. Carrying forward creation myths contributes to stabilize the cultural roots and form a great Shanghai with the strong cultural identity.

Lastly, Shanghai is one of the birthplaces of China's modern mythology studies. The first book on mythology studies in China *Mythology ABC* (1928) 神话学 ABC was written by Mr. Liuyi Xie of The Great China University (which was later combined with Kwang Hua University to form East China Normal University) and published in Shanghai. Mr. Mao Dun's *Chinese Mythology Research ABC* (1929) 中国神话研究 ABC was also written and published in Shanghai. The works of Mr. Lü Simian and Mr. Yang Kuan when they were at Kwang Hua University have contributed greatly to the study of mythology. Therefore, Shanghai has been home to mythological studies.

Therefore, Shanghai being at the right place at the right time with the right people has its advantages in cultivating interests in mythology studies. As a result, we can find that academia pays attention to creation myths study, the government supports it, and the public loves the stories of creation myths.

What are creation myths? Most scholars agree that they are myths about the creation of the world and mankind. It is correct but not sufficient. Our past understanding of the creation myth was one-sided. Why? The world and man were created. But if humans do not have the ability to create the material, spiritual and institutional world, what would differentiate them from animals? Those semi-god creator stories about the inventions of fire, clothing, house, pottery, boat, and wheeled-vehicle, as well as the marriage system, rites, and music system, nine-continent system, let alone those myths of creations of the music culture, filial piety culture, and belief systems; they all belong to creation myths.

Without the creation of heaven and earth, lives will have nowhere to grow; without the birth of humans, there will be nothing; without the invention of objects, mankind would not progress; without the establishment of institutions, the society would have been scattered; without the cultivation of culture and spirit, man will have no soul. So we believe that creation myths should contain the following five categories:

The myths of the creation of heaven and earth
The myths of the birth of humans
The myths of the invention of objects
The myths of institutional establishment
The myths of spiritual cultivation.

Therefore, the creation myth is a sacred narrative when human thinking reaches a higher level and the social development moves to a higher stage with the significance of connecting the past and future for civilization development. The creation myth embodies the unity of a nation's culture, the integration of society, the systematicness of thinking, and the standardization of ethical norm. The creation myth has the significance of laying the foundation of civilization and is the core cultural symbol of national self-identity. Meanwhile, the creation myth can help spread a culture; it is the core field of cultural exchanges and competitions.

After defining the types of creation myths, let us look at what constitutes the creator gods. We believe that myths about the creation of heaven, earth, the sun, and the moon are the very core of creation myths. Heaven and earth produced the entire world. All things originated from heaven. The greatest virtue of heaven and earth is to bring survival and life reproduction. When we return to common sense, we will realize that all things and humans cannot live without heaven and earth. As the gods of reproduction, the sun and the moon played an important role in the creation of man. There have been rich descriptions about the origin of man and all things in ancient narratives. Among them, the great god *Shangdi* 上帝 (the Chinese god), who was derived from heaven, has been an active worship figure on the altar from ancient times to the late Qing Dynasty. Just as the name *Yuandan* 元旦 (literally means *the day of the beginning*, it also used to refer to *the New Year's Day in Chinese Lunar Calendar*) was yielded to the New Year's Day in the western calendar, the name *Shangdi* is generally identified as "God" from abroad. *Shangdi* is an extremely important Chinese cultural heritage that we need to study and inherit. The totem gods such as animal gods and plant gods: the Azure Dragon (*Qinglong*), the White Tiger (*Baihu*), the Black Tortoise (*Xuanwu*) and the Vermilion Bird (*Zhuque*), all belong to the second category of the great creator god. The third category is the ancestor heroes who had served people, such as Fuxi, Nüwa, the Yan Emperor, the Yellow Emperor, Yao, Shun, Gun and Yu the Great. Thus, the creator gods can be put in the following three major categories:

The nature creator god of heaven, earth, the sun, and the moon
The totem creator god of animals and plants
The ancestor creator god of moral heroes.

The three categories above have some overlaps but they are three distinctive categories in Chinese creation myths. That is a special feature of the Chinese creation myths. In order to express more clearly and reflect our thinking, we have made such a distinction between creation myth and creation deities according to the two different standards of creation function and creation god.

The creation mythology is a sacred narrative, which cannot be separated from the three narrative forms: language, ritual behavior, and landscape. Unlike some myths that only have written records left, the Chinese creation mythology is breathing and developing. To a great extent, it is dependent on the folk traditions to be carried down till today. In the narrative of Chinese creation myth, there usually have a magnificent sacred palace, thousands of millions of pilgrims, related festivals and celebrations, which formed the grand folk traditions from generation to generation.

At this time, it reminds me of Mr. Xie Liuyi's conclusion: mythology is folklore, folklore is mythology. Therefore, the study of creation myth must include three methodologies: language exegesis, field investigation of folk behaviors and archaeological analysis of artifacts. In the digital age, the study of the creation myth also needs attention to multi-media and cultural creative industries. Today's academic research needs both traditional skills and modern visions.

Our efforts were just like throwing a brick to attract jade. We hope more and more scholars would be encouraged to join us in studying and passing on Chinese creation myths, because its study has been far less successful than that of the Greek and Roman mythology. We hope that through our efforts, Chinese creation mythology will be accepted by the public and loved by people all over the world.

March 2018 Zhaoyuan Tian
Shanghai, China

The original version of the book was inadvertently published with a few errors. The correction to the book is available at https://doi.org/10.1007/978-981-15-5928-0_7

Contents

1 Heaven, Earth, the Sun, and the Moon: Chinese Nature Myths   1
2 The Creation of Man and Things: Chinese Creation Myths 23
3 The Flying Dragon and the Dancing Phoenix: Chinese Totem
   Myths 43
4 Emperors Yan and Huang, Our Ancestors: Chinese Ancestor
   Myths 75
5 Sages Yao and Shun: Chinese Sage Myths 105
6 Gun and Yu Control the Waters: Chinese Flood Myths 139
Correction to: Myths of the Creation of Chinese C1

Chapter 1
Heaven, Earth, the Sun, and the Moon: Chinese Nature Myths

Zhaoyuan Tian

①Professor Zhaoyuan Tian holds a Ph.D. in History. He is Professor in Folklore Studies, doctoral supervisor, and Associate Dean of the School of Social Development in East China Normal University. He also serves as Director of Regional Cultural Resources and Applied Research Center of East China Normal University, which is affiliated with National Folk Literature and Art Development Center of the Ministry of Culture. Professor Tian is mainly engaged in mythology studies with a focus on folk beliefs, folklore and the culture industry. He is currently an executive member of the Chinese Folklore Society and a member of the Shanghai Intangible Cultural Heritage Protection Expert Committee.

Each of ethnic groups has its own original mythology. Mythology is the source and foundation of a culture, and it records the history of a nation. Mythology is also the history of thoughts. Although mythology does not include the history of early civilization in its entirety, it can draw a rough historical outline. Nature mythology of China can be regarded as father of humanity in the country, as it gave rise to many philosophical thoughts. Today, our topic is creation mythology, which has also received a lot of attention from the cultural management authority of Shanghai Municipal Government. Prior to this, several university professors and scholars with doctoral degrees jointly wrote a book titled *Creation Myths of China* for Juvenile and Children's Publishing House. People thought that having several professors write this book for children was like using a sledgehammer to crack a nut. But, it was a well-written book, and this practice was a worthy endeavor. Later, authorities convened artists to create images about China's ancient creation mythology. Several professors at Fudan University wrote popular articles under this topic. And here, we have several scholars specializing in mythology studies to discuss relevant topics. In these public lectures, we strive to provide different perspectives.

If a nation does not have confidence in its own culture, its development will be restricted; so we should build such confidence. In the past, when the Chinese talked about mythology, Greece had always been put in the forefront whereas China had been considered as a follower. While it is true that Greek culture is most known for its mythology, which is the origin of Western culture, why do people think that our

Chinese mythology is eclipsed in comparison? That is an expansive question. *The Iliad* and *The Odyssey* that people have held in esteem were actually not this long when first written; they have been slowly developed and expanded to what we know at present. The collection of Greek myths which was compiled by the German writer Schwab over a hundred years ago, is also a processed product. It seems that Chinese mythology is actually richer and deeper than Greek's, especially if we include the mythology after the Qin and Han dynasties. More importantly, Chinese mythology is still breathing and developing, which is the most fascinating thing about it. We must take on the project of exploring the origin of Chinese mythology as an approach to revitalize Chinese culture and enhance national confidence. To build confidence in Chinese culture, we must first have confidence in Chinese mythology.

This time, we have three mythology scholars to conduct lectures. There will be six sessions in total.

Heaven, earth, the sun, and the moon are part of the Nature mythology of the Chinese. In China, if one is criticized as not knowing heaven, earth, the sun, and the moon, it means that one does not know the relevant social rules, etiquettes, or the very basics of being a person in society. That is a folk expression. On the other hand, if one keeps talking as if they understand everything, people will ridicule him as the "heaven-understanding god 懂天神". In other words, one cannot know everything about heaven, earth, the sun or the moon; and we are always exploring. How can anyone understand heaven? A person who keeps babbling about heaven, earth, the sun, and the moon is generally considered to be mentally problematic. Now I am in a difficult situation as I think of it. If I say I don't understand the sun or the moon, why should I come here? But if I say that I understand them very well, then it makes me look too self-righteous and arrogant. Does that not make me a "heaven-understanding god"? Today, I am here to exchange opinions with you all and I am doing so with awe. I will try to present my understanding of this esteemed part of Chinese culture and get some feedback, as there may be many learned people in the audience. After all, we are in Shanghai, a place with many talented people.

I am a folklore researcher. Folklore study focuses on the issues of national identity and country identity. It contributes to the development of local economy, and the protection of cultural heritage. Mythology is a form of folklore and a resource for constructing folk identity.

The ancient Chinese rarely used the concept of mythology 神话 *shenhua*. The word is said to have appeared during the Ming dynasty. About a hundred years ago, when the Japanese used Chinese characters to interpret Western mythology, they used the same term *shenhua*. We liked it, so we adopted this word. That was around the beginning of the 20th century. According to the existing records, Liang Qichao was the first person to use *shenhua* as it is used in modern mythology studies. In 1913, Jiang Guanyun published an article "Characters Created through Mythological History 神话历史养成之人物 *Shenhua lishi yangcheng zhi renwu*." We see that *shenhua* was used in the title. With the publication of this article, the modern concept of mythology spread in China. Some people might ask, since we pay so much attention to mythology and legends, why don't we have the same regard for real history? This is an interesting question. We are not ignoring real history. On the contrary, we attach great importance to mythology *and* history, as both are important cultural resources. Mythical imaginations in history and genuine history are of equal value. The spirituality and idealism expressed in mythology are abstracted from reality, and they inspire the reality moving forward.

Mythology is an important part of international communication. The capability of working had been considered as a way to distinguish human beings from animals. But later we found that animals could work as well at some level. Then we thought only human beings were able to use tools, but we gradually found that animals were also capable of using tools. Those were from the perspective of acquiring materials. If labor is an act of material acquisition, then mythology is spiritual. After evolutionary breakthroughs, human beings were able to have imagination based on the existing world; this is a huge leap in thinking. Mythology, rich in imagination, is an extraordinary derivative of thoughts.

Mythology is the eternal home to the ideal and spirit of mankind, and it has always accompanied human beings. In the past, it was believed that mythology was the result of the undeveloped science in the prehistoric era; with more understanding of science, mythology would disappear. Many people thought that after we invented telegraphs, airplanes, radars, and the Internet, we had our own Thousand-Mile Eyes 千里眼 (a god who can see things thousands of miles away) and Wind-Accompanying Ears 顺风耳 (a god who can hear any sound carried on the wind), so people would stop believing in mythology. While it is true that science is constantly improving, mythology does not entirely arise from the absence of science, and science cannot answer all the questions about mythology. There is a modern myth in Shanghai about the Dragon Pillar supporting the viaduct on Yan'an Road. Starting from the late 20th century, people kept talking about it till the 21st century. The myth was that a monk master helped the construction team overcome the piling issue when laying the foundation. Nowadays, it is still common that some engineering and construction teams invite monks to practice religious rituals when the construction is not going smoothly. Indeed, in large real estate projects with billions of *yuan* at stake, religious rituals help construction workers feel reassured. That is understandable. The pile on Yan'an Road could have hit a rock, so it could not go deeper. Many solutions were proposed. This incident was rendered into numerous stories. Some people say that one day the Master Monk from Jade Buddha Temple (some say Longhua Temple) passed by and chanted a spell after learning what happened. He passed away soon after. Some people say that it was because he gave away the heavenly secret. Viewed today, this story is pure fabrication, but why do people love telling it? Because we believe in the power of the mysterious; it triggers imagination.

What would mankind be like were there no more mythology in the world? The answer is that human beings would not be able to move forward. Mythology is idealized and can guide human beings going forward. It is the carrier and the starting point of the Chinese dream. Some time ago, a TV drama series about Premier Zhou was aired. In this series, Henry Kissinger wanted to exchange samples collected from the moon for some soil and liquid from the Mawangdui tomb with China. Kissinger was impressed by the body-preserving technique two thousand years ago in the Mawangdui era in China, so he wanted to have some samples. Premier Zhou rejected this request, saying that a girl called Chang'e had been to the moon two thousand years ago. As we all know, our spacecraft Chang'e 1 had been launched. Although this is remarkable scientific achievement, it is still not as good as what we imagined. To truly explore the moon as freely as Chang'e, we still need to take big strides in science and technology. Therefore, mythology is always ahead of science and reality, leading humans to realize their ideals step by step. Without mythology, we would lose our imagination and national dreams, which inspire our creativity.

Mythology is not only a reflection of social life, but *is* social life, and an organic component of the society. The piling project for the viaduct reflects that our technology was not well enough. The evaluation of the project is also part of this north-south viaduct project. This project is not just a matter of the engineering team, but a system consisting of both physical and cultural aspects, including myths. What is the value of this myth? That is, it reminds us to remember those viaduct builders. Myths help spread stories about those heroes, giving wings to our history and national spirit. History would be a lifeless thing without mythology. Many historical books are better written than *Records of the Three Kingdoms* 三国志, but none compares to its popularity. *Romance of the Three Kingdoms* 三国演义 adds folk culture and mythology in history, that is why it is so intriguing. One example of folk stories in this book is that Zhuge Liang (famous Chinese strategist in the history) invented Mantou (steam bum) to replace human heads for sacrifice ceremonies in the southeast. This story reflects Zhuge's humanism. Nowadays, southwest China is stable with multiple peoples living harmoniously together, and one reason is that several peoples claim Zhuhe as their ancestor. Without such a story, national integration will be difficult. Mythology is a component of a society, mixed with facts and rumors. It reflects and constructs the social life at the same time. Mythology is a kind of belief, an important resource for purifying social customs and realizing social governance.

Mythology is a kind of sacred narrative and structure. It is a sacred discourse system with narratives at its core. Mythological stories are generally magical and are difficult to be fulfilled by human beings. Therefore, we will feel a sense of admiration or worship, which does not diminish ourselves, but inspires human beings to pursue a higher goal of self-improvement. As our life cannot match that in mythology, we are prompted to reach that realm.

Mythology has three forms of narratives. The first is the oral narrative, which later is recorded in books. The second is the narrative of behavior and performance. For example, people go to Mount Putuo to worship, which tells how efficacious the mountain is. This act is the narrative of behavior and performance. The third is the narrative of the landscape, which includes the sacred expression of images and objects, such as temples and gods. For example, if you visit the West Lake, some sites, such as the Broken Bridge, would remind you of the story of Madame White Snake and Xu Xian. Such landscape tells people about a myth. Now there is digital mythological narrative, the Internet mythology, or the digitalization of new and traditional myths. When people are unable to make it home for the Dragon Boat Festival and the Qingming Festival, they would worship their ancestors online. This is a new narrative in the Internet age. Mr. Liuyi Xie said that mythology is folklore, folklore is mythology, and many stories in folklore are mythical narratives. For example, the myth about the Dragon Boat Festival, that Qu Yuan sending a dream saying the sacrifices for him was eaten by fish, is an oral narrative of mythology. People throwing *Zongzi* (rice dumpling wrapped with bamboo leaves) into the river is a behavior narrative of mythology. During a dragon boat race on the Dragon Boat Festival, you will see people displaying Qu Yuan's statues, and throwing *Zongzi* into the river, among a series of other activities. Language, behaviors, and landscapes constitute all aspects about mythology.

Some ethnic groups believe that life spans of animals and humans were arranged by heaven. Once upon a time, Man was late for receiving the life span arrangement from heaven. Dog went early and he received 60 years, while Man only received seven years. Neither was satisfied. Dog didn't want to live that long, and Man did not want to live so short, so the two discussed to exchange their lifespans. Dog proposed a condition that Man has to provide food and shelter to Dog, which Man agreed. From then on, the human being can live for more than sixty years old, and dogs can only live for about seven years old. Dogs and the human beings are in a very harmonious relationship. Mythology is an interpretation and a construction of life.

Below we talk about the system of the mythology about heaven, earth, the sun, and the moon.

In China, such mythology has formed a complete narrative even for children. This narrative is a holistic system centered on heaven. It is also at the very core of Chinese culture. *Thousand Character Classic* 千字文, a primer of Chinese characters for children, started with the four images:

Sky is dark, earth is yellow, and the universe is expansive.
The sun rises and sets, the moon waxes and wanes, and the stars spread all over the sky.

天地玄黄,宇宙洪荒。
日月盈昃,辰宿列张。

A while back, the swimming athlete Yuanhui Fu famously said, "I have used the prehistoric power," and "prehistoric power" became an Internet buzzword. In fact, *Thousand Character Classic*, which has been circulating for one or two thousand years, started by describing the initial state of heaven, earth, the sun, and the moon. Another children's encyclopedia, *Youxue Qionglin* 幼学琼林, also opened with similar topics:

As the chaotic universe was opened,
The heaven and the earth began its formation.
The light and clear air floated up to form the heaven,
And the heavy and dull air solidified into the earth.
The sun, the moon, Venus, Jupiter, Mercury, Mars, and Saturn are called the Seven Stars.
Heaven, earth, and people are called the Three Ways.
The sun governs all the *yang*, and the moon symbolizes *yin*.

混沌初开,乾坤始奠。
气之轻清上浮者为天,
气之重浊下凝者为地。
日月五星,谓之七政;
天地与人,谓之三才。
日为众阳之宗,月乃太阴之象。

We can tell that the knowledge about heaven, earth, the sun, and the moon is quite basic, which children in the past all had to learn by heart.

But this knowledge comes from the national sacrificial system since the pre-Qin period. How did we worship heaven? *Book of Rites* 礼记 says, burning firewood on the altar, burning horses, cattle and other sacrifices, is used to worship heaven; burying the sacrifices is to worship the earth. This is the sacrifice. After the animals are burned, aroma will come out. It communicates with heaven through the smell. Heaven then is aware that people are offering sacrifices to him, and he will send his blessing to humans. 燔柴于泰坛, 祭天也; 瘗埋于泰折, 祭地也; 用 骍犊 People imagined that the most direct connection with heaven was through smell. In the past, people would place a bowl of fresh blood on ceremonies, which produced a blood smell. In the prehistoric age, people thought the blood was the freshest thing. People also felt that the sense of touch could convey messages. For example, they would touch the head of a stone turtle to wish for good luck; and touch the behind of a god statue to wish for a lifetime free of sickness. So the heads of the stone turtles in many places are very smooth. There is also visual communication. People sometimes danced to the god and thought that the god could see it. Another form is the auditory communication. People would recite poems in front of the god. What is important is the material offering, such as sacrifices, meat such as beef or lamb, vegetarian food, flowers, even treasured jade. In short, it must be good things that were offered to the god. Devoted believers even killed their own children to offer to the god. That is, of course, an extreme example. The important thing is that the communication between humans and the god must be sincere. Therefore, people resort to all forms of sacrifices to communicate with their god: olfactory, tactile, visual, auditory, material, and spiritual.

So, to worship the earth, people usually bury good sacrifices. This is to thank the earth for the harvest.

Emperors used to pay tribute to the sun, and the moon. These were royal ritual activities. According to *Book of Rites: Interpretation of Scriptures* 礼记·经解, the Son of Heaven shares the same status as heaven and the earth, so his virtues should match those of heaven and the earth to benefit all things; he is as bright as the sun, and the moon, and his light touches the four seas without missing the minute and the trivial 天子者, 与天地参, 故德配天地, 兼利万物; 与日月并明, 明照四海而不遗微小. The point is not to take advantage of heaven and earth, but to have virtues that are comparable to them. We used to attack the notion of destiny because it is problematic. But we should never dismiss the belief related to heaven, the earth, the sun, and the moon. Even the emperors need to learn virtues of heaven and earth, which is to nurture everything with wind, rain, thunder, and lightning. Emperors should maintain a clean and just political environment for not only the powerful and the wealthy, but for all people; just like the sun, and the moon cast their light to everyone. *Book of Rites*, as an ancient classic, discusses heaven, earth, the sun, and the moon in exactly this order: these four elements are our examples.

What is the heaven exactly? We are not sure. For a long time, it is just an abstract idea. In Christianity and Buddhism, there are god images. For Islamism, there is none. Does the Chinese sky deity have an image? It has always been obscure, but the sun and the moon can be represented by some images. "The ritual pays respect to heaven by worshipping the sun and the moon, which have their designated places in the east and the west, respectively 郊之祭, 大报天而主日, 配以月。祭日于坛, 祭月于坎, 以别幽明, 以制上下。祭日于东, 祭月于西, 以别外内, 以端其位." This establishes order and constructs time and space.

After emperors learned the spirit and virtues of heaven and earth, they needed to understand the social order through the sun and the moon. In other words, the social order was learned from the natural orders of heaven, earth, the sun, and the moon. "The sun rises from the east, and the moon rises from the west. The constant interchange between yin and yang leads to harmony under heaven 日出于东,月生于西,阴阳长短,终始相巡,以致天下之和." How to realize a harmonious society? We can learn it from the harmonious order in heaven and earth. *The Book of Rites* 礼记 is an important book. It is a book of social rules and myths. Heaven, earth, the sun, and the moon constitute a complete framework, which emperors used to build social orders. In the past, there was a question of whether or not to share the resource of Chinese mythology with the general public. How to turn the emperors' privilege to a common belief of the people? In history, it had been difficult for people to participate in a heaven sacrifice, while local governments or even families played major roles in earth sacrifices. Similarly, the sun sacrifice turned from a universal belief to the emperors' privilege; and the moon mythology had been popular among people, although the moon had been a symbol of the queen. So heaven and the sun are in the same category, and their worship is mainly conducted by emperors; earth and the moon are in the same category, and are worshiped among the people as well.

The mythology of heaven, earth, the sun, and the moon gave rise to the construction of social order. In the past we criticized hierarchy, because in nature, we are equal in spirit and rights. But in reality, people have different capabilities and conditions, which create hierarchy in reality. For example, there is hierarchy in economic conditions and power. Without hierarchies, a society would lack momentum. The key question is whether such hierarchies can be changed through efforts in certain conditions. In the continuous development of the Chinese history, a very important drive is class and hierarchy. Just as the constant geographical changes, social hierarchies often change, sometimes for political reasons, some because of individual efforts and opportunities.

As *Book of Rites* goes, things keep moving and integrating without stop, thus music flourishes 流而不息, 合同而化, 而乐兴焉. The rhythm in heaven and earth is indeed like music: "Seeds are planted in spring and grow in summer. This shows the benevolence of heaven and earth. They are harvested in the fall and stored in winter. This shows the justice of heaven and earth 春作夏长, 仁也。

秋敛冬藏，义也." Different virtues are highlighted in a natural order, which is an important piece of wisdom. The Chinese culture stresses the union of heaven and people, which started from here. "In music, harmony is stressed, which follows the rules of heaven; in rituals, difference is stressed, which follows the rules of earth 乐者敦和，率神而从天;礼者别宜，居鬼而从地." Here we can see the difference between music and rituals. "Therefore, a saint should compose music that corresponds to heaven, and design rituals that correspond to earth. With music and rituals in place, heaven and earth can be said to have fulfilled their responsibilities 故圣人作乐以应天，制礼以配地。礼乐明备，天地官矣." Music and rituals also differentiate people's status: "Heaven is high, and earth is low, which determines the positions of the emperor and his subjects 天尊地卑，君臣定矣。卑高已陈，贵贱位矣." In fact, high and low only refer to different positions. "The essence of earth rises, and the essence of heaven falls. *Yin* and *yang* rub against each other, and heaven and earth communicate through thunder, lightning, wind, and rain. Motivated by the four seasons, warmed by the sun and the moon, all creatures flourish. Thus, music is the harmony of heaven and earth 地气上齐，天气下降，阴阳相摩，天地相荡，鼓之以雷霆，奋之以风雨，动之以四时，暖之以日月，而百化兴焉。如此，则乐者天地之和也." This sense of order is very important. China's development is related to order, which is a natural representation of differences.

Where is heaven? As an abstract existence, it is actually an advantage, because its development will not be limited. The Chinese believe that heaven is an omnipresent supreme master. "Heaven is watching people's moves." If this is true, it will restrict our behaviors. People feel that the circle is more in line with the presentation of heaven's omnipresence, so the symbol of heaven is a circle.

The venue of sky-worshipping 5,000 years ago showed that people set fire in a high mountain to pay tribute to heaven (see Fig. 1.1). The notion of a round heaven has been passed on for a long time into the Ming and Qing dynasties, and today.

The Temple of Heaven of the Ming and Qing dynasties reflects inheritance of the heaven belief from the prehistoric age: the Temple is round, which has been the symbol for heaven. As heaven worship was not allowed among people, we do not have a strong affiliation with the round shape. The idea of round-shaped heaven is mainly circulated in royal families (see Fig. 1.2).

Is the heaven a round-shaped surface? No, it is not. Heaven has nine levels, so it is a three-dimensional existence. Qu Yuan asked in *Heavenly Questions*: who created these nine levels? This indicates that in the Warring States period, the mythology of nine levels of heaven had been popular.

In myths and legends, the heaven was supported by eight pillars. Where were these pillars? Qu Yuan asked. But that was from myths, and theoretically it did not exist. In ancient days, transportation had not been well developed so it was impossible to travel around in exploration of this question. However, many places in China are named Tianzhu (sky pillar) Mountain, such as the ones in Anhui, Changyang of Hubei, Shanxi, Fujian, Shandong, and Gansu. There were almost eight pillars! Many of these mountains were named "sky pillar" because they were related to the idea of heaven being supported by pillars, which could be found in myths such as Gonggong

1 Heaven, Earth, the Sun, and the Moon: Chinese Nature Myths

Fig. 1.1 An altar of the Red Mountain culture

Fig. 1.2 Temple of Heaven in Beijing

(the water god) breaking one of pillars as he smashed his head on Mount Buzhou, and Nüwa cutting off a turtle's legs to re-establish these pillars.

So how was the earth placed? According to ancient Chinese mythology, the earth is hung on ropes from heaven. This statement emphasizes the dependence between heaven and earth. Heaven was supported by the pillars on the earth, so it would not fall down, and the earth was pulled by the heaven, so the ground would be solid. Such description cannot stand the scrutiny of reasons, but the concept of heaven and earth being one is fully embodied in this myth. The positions of heaven and earth became the basis of social hierarchy. Therefore, the theory of destiny has long dominated people's mind.

But this order was destroyed by a god called Gonggong. According to ancient mythology, after Gonggong was defeated by Zhuanxu in their fight for the throne, Gonggong lost his temper, smashed his head on Mount Buzhou, and broke this sky pillar, so heaven fell on the northwest side. So did the sun, the moon, and the stars. Another consequence was that the rope tied to the east side of the earth was broken, so the earth sunk on the east, and water flew to the southeast. This myth explains the natural geography that can be observed from the Central Plains in China: rivers flow to the east. The sun, the moon and the stars rise from the east and set in the west: that is as much a natural rule as a potential myth for geographical politics. In ancient Chinese society, northwest China had the political geographical advantage.

The myths about heaven are abundant. There is a complete narrative system about heaven, earth, the sun and the moon. Our current explanation of the universe is the big bang theory. Is this scientific? Who knows? Scientists only have this assumption. While we have scientific assumptions and discussions, please do not ignore the mythological ideas about heaven and earth.

Let's take a look at southeast China. Shanghai, as one of the birthplaces of ancient Chinese civilization, can be found in the narrative of the heaven-and-earth mythology. "The blue *bi* is for heaven, and the yellow *cong* is for earth 苍璧礼天, 黄琮礼地." The Liangzhu culture, which is close to Shanghai, gave a specific image to the heaven god. Heaven was no longer just a circle. Six thousand years ago, heaven god might be like this (see Fig. 1.3), as if wearing a pair of glasses. Traces of fire were found on the top of Fuquan Mountain in Shanghai. Some people think it was left from a sacrifice to the heaven god.

The jade *cong* and *bi* used in sky sacrifice in the Liangzhu culture were often found in archeological discoveries in Shanghai, indicating that this place had a common mythological narrative of heaven and earth.

What other names have been used for China's heaven? One was *shangdi* 上帝. In China, *shangdi* is one with heaven. *Book of Rites: Kings' Systems* 礼记·王制 said, "When the son of heaven goes to war, he should pay tribute to *shangdi*, the nation, and gods 天子将出,类乎上帝,宜乎社,造乎祢." It is about worshipping *shangdi*, or heaven. This leads to our heaviest question today: where is *shangdi* now after having influenced China for five thousand years?

According to *Book of Rites: Moon* 礼记·月令, "the sons of heaven pray for harvest to *shangdi* on the first day of the new year. 天子乃以元日祈谷于上帝." Although

Fig. 1.3 The heaven god in the Liangzhu culture

the first day of the year fell on different dates in Xia, Shang, and Zhou dynasties, people prayed to *shangdi* on the New Year's day, respectively.

When emperors offered sacrifices to heaven, their garment bore symbols of heaven. According to *The Book of Rites: the Suburbs* 礼记·郊特牲, "On the day of sacrifice, the king wore the ritual garment with symbols of heaven. The flags had twelve ribbons, and the royal robe had the sun and the moon patterns to symbolize heaven. All things originated from heaven, and people originated from their ancestors. Therefore, ancestors and heaven were worshipped at the same time 祭之日, 王被衮以象天;旗十有二旒, 龙章而设日月, 以象天也。万物本乎天, 人本乎祖, 此所以配上帝也." The symbols of heaven were used in *shangdi* worship: heaven and *shangdi* were one, so *shangdi* was also known as *Haotian* (vast sky) *Shangdi* 昊天上帝. Later, *Comprehensive Institutions: Rituals* 通典·礼典 stated: "Haotian Shangdi is called thus, because 'haotian' meant expansive vital energy. The one that people respect the most is *di* (the emperor), who is likened to *tian* (heaven), so heaven is also known as *shangdi* (up emperor). 所谓昊天上帝者, 盖元气广大则称昊天, 远视苍苍即称苍天, 人之所尊, 莫过于帝, 托之于天,故称上帝. This clearly explains the relationship between *shangdi* and *tian*."

"All things originated from heaven," this is a fundamental proposition in creation mythology, that is, everything was created by heaven, and by *shangdi*. So, paying tribute to heaven is showing gratitude to our creator. Our studies in creation mythology have overlooked this point, which should be corrected. Heaven and ancestors were worshipped together in the sacrificing ceremonies of *shangdi*, who had been an actual existence in people's mind. For example, *The Book of Songs* 诗经 contained a piece that went: "Emperor Wen in heaven, oh how brilliant he looks. Although the Zhou state is old, its manifest destiny is renewed. With a promising future, Zhou has the blessing of god. Rise and fall, Emperor Wen's soul always stays by the side of god 文王在上, 于昭于天。周虽旧邦, 其命维新。有周不显,帝命不时。文王陟降, 在帝左右." After Emperor Wen passed away, he went to heaven and stayed by the side of the highest authority, *shangdi*, or god.

From the pre-Qin to the Qing dynasty, there were thirteen major rituals, and twelve secondary ones annually. The worship of *shangdi* was a major ritual, together with harvest, rain, and earth, among others 大祀十有三: 正月上辛祈谷, 孟夏常雩, 冬至圜丘, 皆祭昊天上帝;夏至方泽祭皇地祇;中祀十有二: 春分朝日, 秋分夕月. When Christianity arrived in China, "God" was translated as Master of Sky 天主. Later, Ricci took *shangdi* from Chinese to translate "God". After the Qing dynasty was overthrown, so was god. China became a country without god, and *shangdi* that had existed for five thousand years was also gone.

Yuandan 元旦 was the best day in China, and we used this name to refer to the New Year's in the western calendar. We yielded the name of *shangdi* to Christianity, but lost it in our own context. That poses a serious problem. Flipping through our history, never had there been a dynasty when the emperor stopped worshipping heaven and *shangdi*. In fact, every emperor had to pay respect to *shangdi* before he took the throne. China's heaven and *shangdi* mythology is closely related to the sacrifice rituals and the celebrations of the beginning of the year, as well as the knowledge of nature and the universe. So, we must claim intangible cultural heritage to better protect and promote it.

Next, let's talk about the mythology of earth.

According to *Book of Rites*, "The *she* shrine is used to worship earth. Earth carries everything, and heaven gives people omens. People take their fortunes from earth, and make laws according to heaven, so people respect heaven and feel close to earth, and use nice sacrifices to return earth's favors 社所以神地之道也。地载万物, 天垂象。取财于地, 取法于天, 是以尊天而亲地也, 故教民美报焉." People worshiped earth god to pay back earth's nourishment. Earth supports everything. Without earth, the creations of heaven would have nowhere to stay. So we say that heaven gives birth to creatures, and earth raises them; both are indispensable. Therefore, earth god or *she* god is an important creation god.

Heaven represents *yang*, and earth *yin*. Although the popular belief is that too much *yin* is not good, but *yang* without *yin* is not desirable, either. So "the son of heaven's *she* shrine must be exposed to fog, dew, wind, and rain, in order to communicate with heaven and earth 天子大社必受霜露风雨, 以达天地之气也." The *she* shrine must be outdoors without any cover. "Therefore, the overthrown dynasty's *she* shrine shall be covered from the sun." Enemy's *she* shrine also contained aura, and people did not dare to tamper with it. After the Shang dynasty overthrew Xia and held the enthronement ceremony at Xia's shrine, someone suggested removing it. But Tang, the emperor objected and wrote an article titled "Xia Shrine 夏社", saying that it should not be removed because Shang and Xia shared the same shrine. According to *Records of the Grand Historian*, after Emperor Wu of the Zhou dynasty suppressed the last Shang emperor, he had people sweep and clean the Shang's shrine, and reported to heaven that he replaced Shang and enforced justice on behalf of heaven. In fact, Shang's shrine was inherited from the Xia dynasty. After Zhou was established, they built their own shrine. But they dared not remove Shang's shrine, so they covered it with a shed. Earth shrine had to be exposed to the sun to remain its vitality. After it was covered, it only served a symbolic purpose.

1 Heaven, Earth, the Sun, and the Moon: Chinese Nature Myths

Fig. 1.4 A sacrifice tablet for the God of the Soil

The state had value land ownership, and claimed all the land under heaven. In the same vein, earth sacrifice attached great importance. The shrine built by a king for all the people is called the Great Shrine; the one for himself is called the King's Shrine. The shrines built by dukes are called the State Shrines; the ones for themselves are called the Dukes' Shrines. The shrines built by the rank of literati and below are called Zhi Shrine. Gentlemen and ordinary people may have ancestral or earth god tablets 王为群姓立社, 曰大社。王自为立社, 曰王社。诸侯为百姓立社, 曰国社。诸侯自立社, 曰侯社。大夫以下, 成群立社曰置社。庶士、庶人立一祀, 或立户,或立灶." That is related to land ownership. After land became privately owned, many places began to pay respect to God of the Soil (see Fig. 1.4).

Who is the God of the Soil? He is Gonggong's son, named Houtu, or Goulong. Many scholars believe that he is Yu the Great (see Fig. 1.5). Yu was the first-generation God of the Soil, who has been very much revered. Later, more town literati and local gods joined the ranks and assumed the positions of Lord of the Soil and Goddess of the Soil. The God of the Soil can be found in the south and the west, but is rarely seen in Shanghai. Why is that? In Shanghai, you might hold a deed, but it is hard to feel the land. Everybody lives in tall buildings, and land disappears from our horizon.

The belief in God of the Soil is directly related to land ownership. In Macau, you can find sacrifices to God of the Soil at every door. Once I went to Macau, and found God of the Soil and Fortune in front of every door. Curious about whether people on the sixth floor had it, I entered a building, and found that God of the Soil and Fortune was placed by every door, regardless which floor it was. The statue was lighted by electronic lights, and remained on in the night. In addition, God of the Soil was found

Fig. 1.5 Yu the great as God of the Soil

in the front of shrines for other gods. People had to pay respect to God of the Soil before other gods. So God of the Soil was all encompassing. I think that we should have faith in God of the Soil as we enjoy fortunes from land. The money from the skyrocketing house price all comes from land.

Next, I will talk about the sun mythology, which has great influence in China. The sun god is a bird, as shown in Double-phoenix Facing the Sun (7,000 years B.C., Hemudu culture) 双凤朝阳. When designing the symbol for Chinese cultural heritage, we chose the sun god from Chengdu Jinsha relics from over 3,000 years ago. That is a piece of gold with four birds, representing the four seasons. No modern design was its match. The 12 arcs represented twelve months. This is the most representative item for sun worship (see Fig. 1.6).

In Chinese mythology, there is a three-legged bird in the sun, which also appeared in the paintings in the Han dynasty. How come it has three legs? Mainly for stability, perhaps. A two-legged wine cup does not stand firm. In fact, many utensils made of bronze or pottery have three legs (see Fig. 1.7). Some people explain that the third leg represents the penis, which makes some sense, too, as it represents the connection between the holy narrative and the daily life. The rudest curse word is in

Fig. 1.6 Four birds surrounding the sun pattern

Fig. 1.7 Three-legged bird

fact *ri* 日 (sun). Rude as it is, it is also sacred as it was related to reproduction. In folk culture, a ritual is about praying for sons. The family planning policy once restricted this practice. Now facing the aging population, many regions resumed this practice. The narrative about the sun is related to reproduction, so the sun mythology is also important mythology about the creation of the world and human beings.

The sacrifice to heaven and earth is mainly for the sun worship 郊之祭, 大报天而主日. That is Zhou's narrative. The sun worship lasted into the Qing dynasty and the modern times. Even today, people hold ceremonies in the Sun Temple. So the sun worship is carried on (see Fig. 1.8).

Fig. 1.8 The Sun Temple in the Qing dynasty

1 Heaven, Earth, the Sun, and the Moon: Chinese Nature Myths

In my opinion, the purpose of sun worship was clear, which was to wish for light and warmth. According to *Book of Rites: Interpretation of Scriptures* 礼记·经解, the Son of Heaven shares the same status as heaven and earth, so his virtues should match those of heaven and earth to benefit all things; he is as bright as the sun, and the moon, and his light touches the four seas without missing the minute and the trivial 天子者, 与天地参, 故德配天地, 兼利万物;与日月并明, 明照四海而不遗微小.

It is a high standard to require ethics like heaven and earth. To benefit all things means to be benevolent to all things under heaven, does it not? To touch the four seas means to keep a clean and fair political environment, does it not? To not miss the minute and the trivial means to care for the weak, does it not? So the ancient sun worship and the sun mythology represent a political ideology that is derived from the ethics represented by the sun and the moon. Undoubtedly, they are the good traditions that we need to carry on.

The sun exudes a sense of holiness, and so does the moon. People respect the moon because it is a symbol of beauty. The moon mythology is very interesting. First of all, it goes that a toad lives on the moon. Recently, some scholars say that the toad is actually Chang'e, who has a human body and a snake's tail. The toad, dragon snake, and the moon, they three are one (see Fig. 1.9).

The sun and moon mythology cannot be separated in our narrative. The sun is represented by a golden crow, and the moon by a toad. In the past, the crow and the toad always appeared at the same time. But for the appearance of the dragon totem, we would be called the descendants of the bird and the toad. After Yu, the dragon image began to be widely accepted by Chinese and constituted the core creation

Fig. 1.9 Chang'e flying to the moon depicted on the Han stone relief

myth. The dragon belief continued to grow among diversified totems of the Azure Dragon, the White Tiger, the Black Tortoise and the Vermilion Bird. Although the moon was originally related to toad worship, the toad later grew into the dragon's shape. Here, the dragon, the sun and the moon, the toad, and the bird integrated in a magical way.

The sun worship and the moon worship also integrated with the worship of Fuxi and Nüwa. Fuxi was related to the sun, and Nüwa the moon. They hold the sun and the moon respectively, with dragon-shaped tails intertwined, and become the dragon's descendants. This is a major cultural integration, which was completed in the Zhou, Qin, and Han dynasty. The Han stone relief and the Tang painting both vividly depicted the intimate relationship of Fuxi and Nüwa (see Fig. 1.10).

This process shows cultural integration and identity. People of all ethnic groups identify with the mythology of the sun and the moon, and the identity of dragon's descendants, which show the inclusiveness of the Chinese culture. The identification of Fuxi and Nüwa, the sun, the moon, the bird, and the toad as collective cultural symbols is still ongoing, with a long history and expansive geographical coverage. Collective cultural symbols are the Chinese people's pride. In the paintings in Xinjiang in the Tang dynasty, Fuxi has a beard of the Hu people. Multi-ethnic regions have high identification of the dragon, which reflects no trivial issue but cultural identification and the recognition of cultural diversity.

Fig. 1.10 Fuxi and Nüwa in Han stone relief and Tang painting

Fig. 1.11 Moon ritual hosted in East China Normal University on Mid-Autumn Festival

The moon mythology is passed on in folk culture in the form of moon worship on the Mid-Autumn Festival. For example, the students in East China Normal University are engaged in this activity, which is also attended by overseas friends (see Fig. 1.11). The young men provided support only, and did not participate in the ceremony, as tradition had it. Of course, nowadays, there are men burning incense for the moon. In the coming year, during the Fall Equinox or the Mid-Autumn, we plan to perform such ceremony with moon cakes, watermelons, and peanuts to wish for family happiness, peace, and development.

Next, I am going to tell the story of Chang'e. We know that she stole the precious elixir of life from her husband. Another version goes that Chang'e has an affair with her husband's student. A problematic woman, she is. The Chinese people, being tolerant, choose to forgive her, and drew poetic pictures of her flying to the moon (see Fig. 1.12). It shows the generosity of Chinese culture. The moon mythology advocates for loyalty and tolerance. Tolerance is the key to building a harmonious society. The Mid-Autumn Festival provides an opportunity to forgive and adjust relationship. During several lectures at Shanghai Museum, I mentioned that the Mid-Autumn Festival was the females' festival, and so was the Double Seventh Day. The exclusion of males during these holidays show that women's status was sometimes higher in the traditional society because they monopolize a cultural resource. In Shanghai, the wife manages the home in many families, which in fact reflects the leading powers of females.

Fig. 1.12 Chang'e flying to the moon

The mythology about heaven, earth, the sun, and the moon is the epitome of creation mythology, and we put it at the forefront of the Chinese creation myths. Not only because these myths are essential in creation myths, but also they show the distinctive nature of the Chinese creation myths. Heaven, earth, the sun, and the moon are creators of the world and human beings, and their mythology should be shared by everyone.

There has been a balance of power between the government and the people. The heaven sacrifice had been the royal family's privilege, while people were not allowed. But people would plead "my heaven!" when in difficulties, just like the westerners say "my god" when calling for their savior. In the Song dynasty, the two powers were combined as the Jade Emperor appeared as the embodiment of heaven.

Later, the division appeared again and lasted until the Qing dynasty. Today, beliefs in the Jade Emperor and Zhenwu Emperor continue among people, which is also the inheritance of the Chinese *shangdi*. We support the rejuvenation of the heaven-and-earth sacrifice and the belief in *shangdi*. The worship of the God of the Soil is a great cultural heritage.

Mythology about heaven, earth, the sun, and the moon is an enormous cultural legacy that needs to be protected and passed on. We should first pay respects to nature and its order; after that we can strive for harmony, beauty, tolerance, and identity. Our worship to the moon shows our trust in beauty. Such profound legacy has universal recognition, as people from all nations face heaven, earth, the sun, and the moon. That constitutes a basic premise for international cultural exchange. Such mythology should be protected as a part of China's intangible cultural heritage. I wish everyone can inherit and pass on the cultural essence contained in such mythology.

Chapter 2
The Creation of Man and Things: Chinese Creation Myths

Zhaoyuan Tian

Westerners say that Man is created by God and Chinese say that Man is made from mud. Christians believe that men were born with original sins, but with belief, one can atone for his sins; and Chinese mythology tells people that there is a hierarchy that one should gladly abide by the predestined arrangement. Which statement holds the truth? And how should we interpret Chinese mythology?

In the last chapter, we talked about myths about heaven, earth, the sun, and the moon, which are very important parts of the creation mythology. They are the root questions of Chinese culture and are tightly coupled with the real world. Some of the stories touched upon real-life problems that we are very concerned with, and we can relate to mythology in our daily lives.

In this chapter we will talk about the creation of Man and things. This is a topic both interesting as well as serious. How did everything come into being? How was Man created? I'll share my research about the mythology related to these questions.

Mythology is narration about the nature and the society. They are sacred narration created to explain the causal relationship between natural and social phenomenon. Researchers around the globe have published books on mythological philosophy, where the explanations and opinions are based upon practical experiences, instead of being created in a vacuum. Hence, mythology is a reflection of social lives. There are at least two forms of such reflection: the first is consistent with the reality, and second is the opposite: the mythological world is a totally different existence from the reality. Yet, both are based on reality. The former extols the reality, while the latter extols the ideality by revealing the dissatisfaction about the reality. Hence, both reflections show authentic emotions about reality. They came into being naturally and logically, as opposed to coming out of nothing.

Mythology is a part of the social life and culture. Unlike a mirror, those mythological narratives never flatly record what happened in the society. Instead, they influence the social life and become a part of it. Social life consists of institutions and behaviors, as well as narratives that safeguard or subvert such institutions and behaviors. Hence, the social life has two parts: the behavioral part and the cultural part. Mythology is an important part of this social culture. It is a mysterious public opinion that builds or destroys a certain type of existing order. Where am I from? Where am I going? Who am I? These are questions asked in primary and middle schools. How is the world made up and who created it? This mythology discourse is closely related to a certain social order.

Creation myths praise the creators. It is especially significant nowadays when innovation and entrepreneurship are encouraged among people. Innovation and entrepreneurship are what creation myths have been advocating. And people have long spoken highly of creators. Nobel laureates are admired by the public when the Nobel prize is revealed, because it presents the level of scientific research. As Joseph Needham put it in *Science and Civilisation in China*, China had a lot of world-leading creations before capitalism entered modern industrialization. China was left behind during the early modern age, and the question why modern technology was not born in China has been asked for years. From my personal perspective, we cannot create all advanced technologies, as the billions of people all over the world are supposed to contribute as well. Humans learn from each other, hence we learn from others if they are more advanced. However, our enormous research facilities should make our own contributions. We should not look down upon ourselves, since our scientists are indeed hard-working, with fruitful results. Creation myths talk about stories of creation, giving a boost to the environment of creation. Under this cultural environment, the future of China leading the world in science and economy again is promising.

Yesterday I mentioned that mythology gives wings to cultural spirits, and has the power to inspire imagination and communication. Different from historical narrative, mythology always stays ahead of reality and goes beyond history. We used to dismiss mythology as fake stories. This kind of attitude often leads to misunderstanding, and people would develop resistance against such imaginative narrative, and we would make mistakes. It is high time that we talk about the significance of mythology, as the resistance against it will impact our innovation. Mythology has documented the spiritual world of the past, and will push forward the future.

Yesterday we also mentioned that mythology is a mysterious public opinion to both establish and destroy a certain order. For example, we all know that the end of the Eastern Han dynasty saw the spread of a mysterious song: The good fortune of the Han is exhausted, and the Wise and Worthy Man has appeared. Discern the will of Heaven, O ye people, and walk in the way of righteousness, whereby alone ye may attain to peace 苍天已死, 黄天当立, 岁在甲子, 天下大吉. From today's perspective, it is actually a political rumor. Public opinion goes first, followed by armed battles, and the existing social order will be shaken. That is a realistic myth. The Eastern Han regime was struck strongly by the myth along with armed wars. Although the mythological narratives are about unrealistic events, they attempt to affect the reality. Via oral, written, and behavioral channels, and by god statues and images—mythology is a narrative system.

Mythology is a kind of explanation and a philosophical mindset in nature. Creators and narrators of myths are all philosophers and thinkers. Yesterday we talked about the heaven myths, which are about the belief in god, establishment of order, and reverence of nature. These are philosophical and social topics. In the past, mythologists

Fig. 2.1 From left to right: Karl Marx and Friedrich Engels

were also philosophers. Nowadays, philosophers seldom do research on mythology, nor are they interested, despite that they should have this leap in mindset. Karl Marx and Friedrich Engels interpreted mythology as the narration of mankind's childhood which includes both narration of nature mythology and discussion about Greek mythology. Engels discussed social mythology, saying that in Greek tragedy, goddesses lost their status because of the breakdown of matrilineality and rise of patriarchy. With acute insight, he pointed out the world of mythology changes with the change in social status. Marx and Engels are outstanding mythologists (see Fig. 2.1).

Sigmund Freud's psychoanalytic theories, especially the theory of the unconscious mind, are one of the most influential theories. He believes that the unconscious mind has two innate urges to aggression and sex, which are usually suppressed. He proposed the concept of Oedipus Complex. In Greek tragedy, Oedipus was born with a prophecy that he would kill his father and marry his mother. People were afraid of the prophecy and decided to abandon him. He was then adopted by a person from the neighboring kingdom. After he grew up, he had a conflict and killed an elder king, failing to realize that the king was his father. This young guy was good-looking and intelligent, and he was elected as the new king. According to the past tradition, he would marry the queen if he took over the kingdom, hence the queen became his wife. It seemed destined that his prophecy became reality, and this is the tragedy of destiny. Freud believed this thought was in the subconsciousness, thus, this philosopher built his own language system from Greek mythology.

Claude Lévi-Strauss is a master of Structuralism. He proposed the theory of binary oppositions in mythology, such as absence and satisfaction. Let's use this pair of opposition to analyze this Chinese story, the Cowherd and the Weaving Girl. The Cowherd was a bachelor. One day the Weaving Girl came down from Heaven to take a bath in a pond. He wanted her as his wife. His cow told him, "why not hide

Fig. 2.2 From left to right: Sigmund Freud and Lévi-Strauss

one of her beautiful clothes?" He did so, and the Weaving Girl was not able to leave and had to become his wife. There are many ways of reading this. Let's read it by the theory of Lévi-Strauss. First there is absence—the Cowherd needed a wife. Now what he had to do is to satisfy himself by taking control of the Weaving Girl. We can also interpret this story with another pair of opposition: taboo and the breaking of the taboo. The Cow told the Cowherd to hide away the Weaving Girl's fine clothes, or she would put it on and leave. This is a taboo. However, the Cowherd didn't hide it well and so the Weaving Girl found the clothes and left. The story also has many versions. The one in the current teaching material of Chinese for elementary students was written by Shengtao Ye. Other versions go that the Weaving Girl didn't really want to stay because it was a poor family, but she was unable to take flight without the magic dress. Thus, she tried various ways to make her daughter ask the father. Once the daughter figured out where the clothes were and told her mother, the Weaving Girl left immediately with it. This is in perfect consistency with real marriages in ancient times. In no way would a cowherd be able to marry a goddess, a noble girl, which aligns with the reality of the society. There is a taboo of keeping the magic dress hidden. When the Cowherd failed to hide it well, she left. This is very structuralistic and is a typical binary opposition. Lévi-Strauss was able to read this from an original story so he became a master of Structuralism. Whether he was a master or an ordinary scholar, the truth is, his theory was derived from the research of mythology (see Fig. 2.2).

Creation myths praise the creators. We can understand the origin of creation mythology from the perspective of folkloristic. Folk customs, just like a colorful music piece, are created and led by cultural elites, and participated, recognized, and jointly built by the populace. They do not equal to daily life, or popular culture. It is no exaggeration to say that folk customs belong to the highbrow culture, and is something that can elevate the spiritual life. Creation myths are all about heroes and creators; of course, these are stories of elites. So we say that folk customs are created by elites, and told, identified, and even worshiped by the populace, which means folks formed folk customs collectively.

Creation myths refer to the narratives about Man and the earliest creators of the world, which are hero epics and sacred narratives. Folk customs to some extent are the behavioral expression of mythology. Mythology needs to be expressed through actions, such as interaction with deities and ancestors, and by doing so, mythology can live with us. How can mythology be passed on in living forms? Except for word of mouth, mythological heroes are enshrined in temples and commemorated by setting a memorial day, which are two very important things.

Chinese mythology has a principle regarding who can be offered sacrifices. *The Book of Rites* 礼记 clearly states: "Sacrifices should be offered to him who had given (good) laws to the people; to him who had labored to the death in the discharge of his duties; to him who had strengthened the state by his laborious toil; to him who had boldly and successfully met great calamities; and to him who had warded off great evils 法施于民则祀之, 以死勤事则祀之, 以劳定国则祀之, 能御大菑则祀之, 能捍大患则祀之." People who did a lot of good things for the country, brought welfare to everybody, and people who were loyal and responsible, should be offered sacrifices. For example, Yu passed the door of his house three times without entering it because he was busy controlling the flood (see Fig. 2.3). Such heroes who saved the world from catastrophes, should be offered sacrifices. "The son of Lishan Shi (the Yan Emperor) was called Nong. He was managed to produce crops. Thereafter, during the era of Xia, Qi 弃, the ancestor of Zhou continued farming and cropping. So he was offered sacrifice as Ji 稷. 是故厉山氏之有天下也, 其子曰农, 能殖百谷;夏之衰也, 周弃继之, 故祀以为稷." Ji 稷, the agriculture god, who had made great contributions should be offered sacrifices. "Houtu, son of the water god Gonggong was able to put an order in the nine states, so he was honored as the earth god 共工氏之霸九有也, 其子曰后土, 能平九土, 故祀以为社." People also should pay respect to him. The names of the agriculture god and the earth god combined, *sheji* 社稷, was used to refer to the country and sovereignty. "As to the sun, the moon, the stars, and constellations, people look up to them, while mountains, forests, streams, valleys, hills, and mountains supply people with the materials which they need 及夫日月星辰, 民所瞻仰也;山林川谷丘陵, 民所取材用也." Only those who made contributions to the populace should become recipients of sacrifices. So, the god sacrifice itself is a system based on gratitude. The telling of creation myths represents the gratitude and returns to the creators.

Where were we from? The theory of evolution proposed by Darwin believed that humans were evolved from apes, a result of sexual selection. In the world of apes, female apes have the right to choose strong male apes to mate, giving birth to healthy descendants. Thus, the next generation became superior to the previous one. The weak apes do not have rights to mate or reproduce, so they were eliminated. However, people found that female apes would also choose apes that look flawed. For example, some male apes are not very strong, but they are attentive. Their future

Fig. 2.3 Yu tames the flood

descendants may not be very strong, but quite smart. However, the eventual evolution of human beings is not guaranteed. It can be seen that the head ape should have good intelligence and strength to defeat all rivals, which ensures the development of the group.

Engels believed that labor is critical in the transition from ape to man. Our hands and brain became dexterous through labor, and we became able to stand on two feet, gradually evolved into human beings. It is still unclear now that where on earth we were from. Why apes in the past evolved into humans, but apes in the present do not? Science cannot perfectly explain the origin of humans.

According to Western mythology, God created everything. The explanation from the Bible: "In the beginning, God created the heaven and the earth. And the earth was without form, and void; and darkness was upon the face of the deep: and the Spirit of God moved upon the face of the waters. And God said, let there be light: and there was light." Then, on the last day, God created man, and fed him with vegetables and fruits. Adam lived in the Garden of Eden, with gold and agate, murmuring running water, a nice place. God thought Adam was lonely, so he created Eve, a woman.

"This at last is bone of my bones and flesh of my flesh; she shall be called Woman, because she was taken out of Man." In fact, man is born by woman. We found that this Genesis is value-oriented. Naked while not ashamed, this is an important concept. God told them not to eat the forbidden fruit on the tree, or they would know good and evil, and they would have wisdom. The snake came to tempt them, and they had the feeling of shame right away after eating the apple, so they put on clothes. God saw this and punished them, dislodging them out.

Christians in the audience may believe that this is real instead of a myth, which is understandable. However, mythology researchers believe this is a sacred narrative, among different mythological narrations. Man and the things were created by God alone, instead of the products of cooperation; that means that Christianity belongs to monotheism. It is an odd logic that you should not know good and evil, and that it is a sin to know good and evil. How to explain it? Let us put aside this logic of belief and culture, and draw our attention to the motif of taboo in myths and stories: You have to undertake the outcome of violating taboos. This is a simple genre, but it brings a distinctive cultural taste. In this culture community, believing in Christianity is your duty, because you are born with sins. The creation story of humans is the initial outline about certain culture patterns.

The Chinese myth of Nüwa 女娲 creating Man has been spread since the era of *Songs of Chu* 楚辞. Qu Yuan, the author of *Songs of Chu*, asked the question: Nüwa created Man, but who created Nüwa? Of course, myths cannot withstand questions like this, because it is based on belief, not on logic or reality.

The book *Folk Legend* 风俗通义, written in Han dynasty, goes that: "It is said that Man did not exist when the sky was separated from the earth. Nüwa began to make Man out of clay. She worked as hard as she could but she felt it was still not fast enough. So she decided to dip the rope in the clay and flicked it, so blobs of clay landed everywhere and each became a person. Those who were clay figurines became the well-off, and who were the clay blobs became the poor. 俗说:天地开辟，未有人民。女娲抟黄土作人。务剧力不暇供。乃引绳于泥中，举以为人。故富贵者黄土人也，贫贱者，引绳人也." This story tells us that Nüwa made two types of men. One took her a lot of efforts and was finely made, the other was made in a rather simple way. Thus, the destiny of these two types of men are inherently different. This story about making Man is one about social hierarchy. In our society, some are better-off, others are poor, and this was decided before one was born. Some believe that this story was initially created by the ruling class to make sure people were content with the status quo. This narrative is about the social order, and from it we can see that mythology is used as a basis of the status quo (see Figs. 2.4 and 2.5).

But we also found that this story was very likely to be made up by the poor themselves. Due to various reasons, the poor couldn't change their destiny, so they had to accept their fate and believe that they were made of nothing but blobs of clay. So, they were meant to be members of the poor class because Nüwa didn't give them good fortune in the first place. From the perspective of psychology, it could very much be the fact. Field studies have shown that some ethnic groups attribute their less fortunate lives to the claim that when the deity created Man, one ethnic group was made first, who took away all the good stuff. Being the last ones made, there was

Fig. 2.4 Nüwa creating Man

Fig. 2.5 Creation Hall, Xihua, Zhoukou, Henan

nothing left. Therefore, the other group enjoys better lives, all because they had an advantage when created. This is a version of the weak. Whether the story of Nüwa creating Man a narrative by the strong or the weak, there is no decisive answer. Based on my research, it was quite likely a justification of the weak for their status quo.

Rich or poor, all men were created by Nüwa and should be thankful and bow their heads in front of her. The story of Nüwa creating Man was not just a topic about social order, but a narrative peculiar to the Chinese people. Making Man with clay is not only related to the yellow earth that covers most of China's lands, but also the yellow skin of Asians. Also, making clay figurines is a symbol of Chinese handicraft. Therefore, the myth of Nüwa creating Man was not just about social order. It is fundamentally about the creation of lives, and the creation of materials is an equally important question.

According to *Readings of the Taiping Era* 太平御览, Nüwa created chicken on the first day of the first month of the lunar year, dogs on the second day, sheep on the third, pigs on the fourth, horses on the sixth, and man on the seventh. That's why the seventh day of the first month of the lunar year is celebrated as Man's Day. As the creator of all beings, Nüwa did everything by herself, like God. From these stories, Nüwa is an ancient deity and is considered one of the Three Sovereigns.

However, the myth of Nüwa creating Man later evolved into various husband-and-wife versions, and she eventually became the creator of the marriage system. So from the single deity of Nüwa, we had a glance of social evolution. This reflects the uniqueness of Chinese mythology. In the long history, the myth of Nüwa has evolved with the development of society and grown into a rich mythological system.

From creating Man to giving birth to Man, the transition is a special feature of the Chinese creation mythology. From the different versions of an important goddess creating Man, we can sense the openness and extendibility of Chinese creation mythology. On one hand, it reflects different social forms; on the other, it is the product of different ethnic groups combining their local myths and the Nüwa myth after they joined the community.

The goddess Nüwa, who was said to have created Man alone, became the wife of Fuxi 伏羲. This story became mature in the Han dynasty. Uniting the two gods of the Three Sovereigns as a couple, that was the first great change. It was the result of the establishment of the traditional monogamy system. Spousal relationship has been highly valued in the traditional Chinese society, as it can enhance interpersonal relationship and improve education. It was of great significance that Fuxi and Nüwa became the first couple. Nüwa hence became the founder of the marriage system. The image of the Fuxi-Nüwa couple with human heads and dragon bodies, which integrated the narrative of dragon's descendants, the myths of heavens and earth, and the yin-yang orders, and became the most classic expression of the Chinese creation mythology with the most profound messages.

Such creation myth with kings as protagonists became stories of brothers and sisters among the grassroots. The story of Fuxi the brother and Nüwa the sister giving birth to Man carries a trace of consanguineous marriage, while the narrative itself warns people about the taboo of such marriage. Thus we see the following version in the book *Duyizhi* 独异志 in the Tang dynasty:

When the universe was first shaped, Fuxi the brother and Nüwa the sister on Mount Kunlun were the only human beings on earth. Since there were no other people in the world, they discussed and decided to get married to each other; but they felt ashamed. The brother said, if Heaven would agree us to marry each other, please make the smoke merge; if not, please keep it separate. Then the smoke merged. Thus, the sister came to the brother and made a fan with grass to cover her face. Nowadays we have the tradition of wife covering her face with a fan on the wedding, which is a symbolistic act of the legend. 昔宇宙初开之时, 止女娲兄妹二人, 在昆仑山。而天下未有人民, 议以为夫妻, 又自羞耻。兄即与其妹上昆仑山。兄曰:"天若遣我二人为夫妻, 而烟悉合;若不, 使烟散。"于烟即合。其妹即来就兄, 乃结草为扇, 以障其面。今时取妇执扇, 象其事也。

This story is the prototype of many later coming ones about the sibling marriage of Fuxi and Nüwa. In the later versions, the storylines became more complicated. One of the typical plots is rolling the millstone. Because Fuxi and Nüwa, as brother and sister, are not supposed to marry each other, yet humans would go extinct if they don't. Hence after many rounds of testing god's will, they decided to do a final test. They would each hold half of a millstone and go up to the top of two mountains facing each other. Then they would let go of their half and see if the halves would match perfectly when they meet. And so them did, and the two halves matched perfectly, thus they got married. The story also goes that they gave birth to a ball of flesh, which conveyed the physiological harm of sibling marriage. This story is advising against sibling marriage. You may wonder: why only this pair of brother and sister were left? Other stories explained that humans had made mistakes, hence the punishment from heaven. Usually the punishment is a flood. This is the Chinese version of an archetypal story—the Flood. Such plot carries values for comparative cultural studies.

The story of the sibling marriage of Fuxi and Nüwa as common folks, is interestingly different from the story of them as two of the Three Sovereigns, and its impact is even greater than the story of Fuxi and Nüwa with human heads and snake bodies. In the story's later versions, Nüwa was no longer with Fuxi, but was with a more prestigious god — Pangu. Thus, we have the story of Nüwa the sister and Pangu the brother giving birth to Man. From all the stories, we can tell that, Nüwa had been the main character; no matter she created Man alone, or with the dragon, or through marriage,

Among the three major series of the Chinese creation mythology, namely, Man being created by heaven, earth, the sun, and the moon; Man being created by totems; and Man being created by ancestors, Nüwa plays a major and leading role. In this sense, the myth of Nüwa creating Man is the epitome of Chinese creation myths.

Where on earth did Man come from? Different ethnic groups and geographical regions have many narratives. Mythology is told not only as stories, but also through logical expressions. In the *Book of Rites, Chapter Questions of Duke Ai* 礼记·哀公问, Confucius said, "If there were not the united action of heaven and earth, the world of things would not grow 天地不合,万物不生." Heaven and earth must be united before things grow. This leads us back to the mythology of heaven, earth, the sun, and the moon.

2 The Creation of Man and Things: Chinese Creation Myths

The creation of Man, though related to their ancestors, is not going to happen without the union of heaven and earth. The union is the premise of Man being created. "All lives originated from heaven, and all men originated from their ancestors 万物本乎天, 人本乎祖." The book of *I Ching* 周易 says: "Heaven and earth exert their influence, and the transformation and production of all things ensue. Sages influence the minds of man, which leads to harmony and peace all under heaven 天地感而万物化生, 圣人感人心而天下和平." All beings, including Man, were created under the mixed influence of heaven and earth. If it never rains, how could anything survive? If the sun never shines, there won't be any lives. These are proofs of the importance of the exertion of heaven and earth.

"If no intercommunication happened between heaven and earth, things would not grow nor flourish. The great virtue of heaven and earth is called reproduction 天地不交而万物不兴。天地之大德曰生." The most important function of heaven and earth is to produce all beings. This is also referenced as "after heaven and earth took shape, all things were produced. Heaven and earth beget all beings, which beget men and women. From men and women emerged husband and wife, and father and son ensued. From father and son came ruler and minister, thus emerged the superior and the inferior, which led to the arrangements of propriety and righteousness. 有天地, 然后万物生焉。有天地然后有万物, 有万物然后有男女, 有男女然后有夫妇, 有夫妇然后有父子, 有父子然后有君臣, 有君臣然后有上下, 有上下然后礼义有所错." Heaven and earth are the isomorphism of husband and wife, both producing lives.

There are two kinds of narratives about Chinese creation mythology: one is in an intuitive and story-telling style, and the other is philosophical with no plot or details, yet the morals convey profound meanings.

What kind of culture does this kind of philosophical narrative form? Zeng-zi said, "The body is that which has been transmitted to us by our parents; dare anyone allow himself to be irreverent in the employment of their legacy? If a man in his own house and privacy be not grave, he is not filial; if in serving his ruler, he be not loyal, he is not filial; if in discharging the duties of office, he be not reverent, he is not filial; if with friends he be not sincere, he is not filial; if on the field of battle he be not brave, he is not filial. The fundamental lesson for all is filial piety. The practice of it is seen in the support (of parents).[1] 身也者, 父母之遗体也。行父母之遗体, 敢不敬乎?居处不庄, 非孝也;事君不忠, 非孝也;莅官不敬, 非孝也;朋友不信, 非孝也;战阵无勇, 非孝也;众之本教曰孝, 其行曰养." My body is given by my parents, and so is my flesh. In the old days, one should not cut his nails as one pleases, or damage his body, because the body is also part of the inheritance in the family. You might think that everyone has the right to do whatever to his or her own body, which is a modern view. But the old belief makes sense, and provides a very important reason for people to cherish their own body. With this taboo, you cannot destroy your body, otherwise you would destroy the bloodline passed down from the ancestors. It forces you to cherish your body, because it does not belong to you alone, but is the inheritance from our parents. As we observe filial piety, we should go beyond the family level, and

---

[1] Translated by Derk Bodde in *A History of Chinese Philosophy* by Yu-lan Fung.

apply it on the country level. The monarchy hierarchy is not the highest relationship, we need to realize our own value in the society while observing the ethics for married couples. Here, the Book of Rites especially talks about filial piety: "set up filial piety, and it will fill the space from earth to heaven; spread it out, and it will extend over all the ground to the four seas; Hand it down to future ages, and from morning to evening it will be observed; push it on to the eastern sea, the western sea, the southern sea, and the northern sea, and it will be (everywhere) the law for men, and their obedience to it will be uniform. Zeng-zi said, 'Trees are felled and animals killed, (only) at the proper seasons.' The Master (Confucius) said, 'To fell a single tree, or kill a single animal, not at the proper season, is contrary to filial piety.'[2] 夫孝, 置之而塞乎天地, 溥之而横乎四海, 施诸后世而无朝夕, 推而放诸东海而准, 推而放诸西海而准, 推而放诸南海而准, 推而放诸北海而准。曾子曰: 树木以时伐焉, 禽兽以时杀焉。夫子曰:断一树, 杀一兽, 不以其时, 非孝也."

Filial piety needs to become a principle: one must do things in its natural order. For example, you should not cut trees in the spring, or hunt in the breeding season. China's childbirth culture eventually became a love for the whole nature, including honoring parents, respecting kings, and treating animals based on certain rules. Thus, filial piety becomes a very elevated mindset. The Chinese creation myth is not too rich, but contents on respecting ancestors and valuing filial piety are the most detailed. Regarding the creation of Man by heaven, earth and ancestors, we will skip the detailed processes. However, as the saying goes, "on the left is the ancestral shrine, and on the right is the soil and grain," the ancestral shrine is placed at the most important place—very important to respect life and the future. The greatest significance of creation myth is that it highlights filial piety and combines the birth-giving of parents with the great virtues of heaven and earth. Parents' giving birth to children becomes a part of the evolvement of heaven and earth. The creation myth is interpreted by every couple; in a way, the protagonists of the creation myth are each individual. *I Ching* 周易 goes that after heaven and earth took shape, all things were produced. Heaven and earth beget all beings, which beget men and women. From men and women emerged husband and wife, and father and son ensued. From father and son came ruler and minister, thus emerged the superior and the inferior, which led to the arrangements of propriety and righteousness 有天地然后有万物, 有万物然后有男女, 有男女然后有夫妇, 有夫妇然后有父子, 有父子然后有君臣, 有君臣然后有上下, 有上下然后礼义有所错. Isn't it true that husband and wife's giving birth to children correspond the way of heaven and earth, and form the basis of the social order?

Therefore, we found that parents who gave birth to children were as sacred as Nüwa who created Man. They equally deserve our worship. Through the concept of filial piety, a deity is connected to ordinary people, and creation myths become an elevation of personal status. When Fuxi and Nüwa, heaven and earth, the sun and the moon, and husband and wife share the same function, the creation myth becomes something that every individual can take part in. The greatest virtue of heaven and earth is creating Man; together with parents' eternal grace, they form the exquisite narrative structure of mythological philosophy.

---

[2]Translated by John C. H. Wu in *Beyond East and West*.

2 The Creation of Man and Things: Chinese Creation Myths

About Nüwa, there was not only a story of creating Man, but also a myth about brilliant contribution like patching the sky. According to the *Book of Huainanzi, Lanming Chapter* 淮南子·览冥训, "In the ancient times, when four supporting pillars of heaven were discarded and the nine lands of earth were breached. The Heaven could no longer be the cover and earth could no longer be the support. Wildfires spread fast and floods were rampant. Beasts and raptors ate people. It was Nüwa who alchemized the five-colored stones to mend the sky, and hunted a gigantic turtle for its four feet to support the sky. She slaughtered the black dragon to save the lands, and used ashes and mud to stop the floods. With the sky mended and supported, floods died down, dragon killed, and the man could live peacefully again. 往古之时, 四极废, 九州裂, 天不兼覆, 地不周载, 火燻炎而不灭, 水浩洋而不息, 猛兽食颛民, 鸷鸟攫老弱。于是, 女娲炼五色石以补苍天, 断鳌足以立四极, 杀黑龙以济冀州, 积芦灰以止淫水。苍天补, 四极正;淫水涸, 冀州平;狡虫死, 颛民生。"

This story is rich in connotation. It is also a kind of creation myth, that is, the re-creation of heaven and earth. Patching the sky can be regarded as a supplement to the myth of Pangu creating heaven and earth. Rebuilding the sky pillar is also a matter of rectifying the order in heaven and earth. This is a major event, so it is a heroic myth about disasters and salvation. From this story, the myth of craftsmanship was derived. For example, it contained the language of refining the five-color stones, so people working in the smelting industry regard Nüwa as the god of the furnace.

Thus, Nüwa changed from the creator of Man to the creator of artifacts. Xu Shen said in the *Book of Shuowen* 说文: "Nüwa, the sacred goddess of ancient times, the person who cultivated all things 娲, 古之神圣女, 化育万物者也." It is the function of heaven to cultivate everything! But such a great goddess she is: creating Man and things. Legend goes that she created seventy things in one day. According to ancient mythology, Nüwa has a super high status.

Nüwa created the musical instruments of *sheng* 笙 and *huang* 簧, which was an amazing contribution. We found that the creation of Man and creation of things had always been united. Nüwa created man, however she created the rooster first, then the dog, and it was only on the seventh day that she created Man. She also created *sheng* and *huang*, as well as other musical instruments. In the Chinese ritual and music society, the manufacture of musical instruments always came first. You will find that our creation god would always create some sort of instrument: Nüwa created the *sheng* and *huang*, and Fuxi created *qin*. The Yellow Emperor and The Goddess invented the drum together, and they commanded Linglun to create *qing* and Chui to create bells. It seems that all the Chinese traditional percussion instruments were created by the Yellow Emperor. Emperor Yan, or Shennong are creators of *qin* and *se*. Fuxi and Nüwa, the Yan Emperor and the Yellow Emperor, these four ancestors invented percussion instruments, plucked instruments, and wind instruments. *Book of Origins, Chapter Zuo* 世本·作篇 described in great details the creation of these musical instruments, and these creators are our ancient ancestors. This explains why we value the creation of matter, but more so do we value the creation of spiritual wealth. Musical instruments are tightly coupled with the development of the ritual and musical culture of ancient China, and the creation of musical instruments is the basis of rituals.

The Chinese told the creation myths of implements and rituals part in such a solemn tone as if the creators of things and the ritual systems were actual historical figures. *Book of Origins, Chapter Zuo* is the origin of this kind of myth. *Book of Origins* lists the creation of fire in the first place, which shows people's recognition of the importance of fire in the ancient times. Fire changed life; it is a tool to fight the nature. Therefore, from Suiren to Shennong and the Yan Emperor, fire gods are a long list. Today, the worship of the god of fire is still popular in China, which tells the distinctiveness of fire.

Then, *Book of Origins* tells the story of another creator, Fuxi, who created the wedding ceremony rituals. We can see from it that Chinese creation mythology very much values the establishment of systems. Without systems or etiquette, there would be no social order. The creation of systems is very unique to the Chinese creation mythology. The husband-and-wife system is the starting point of the entire Chinese culture; hence it has received great attention. We saw that the traditional wedding ceremony has three worship procedures: firstly, bow to Heaven and Earth; secondly, bow to the parents; and lastly, bow to the spouse. These procedures are very solemn, showing the inheritance of the essence of the ancient creation mythology.

After the wedding ceremony rituals was the creation of instruments. Fuxi created *qin* and *se*, so did Shennong. It seems that *qin* and *se* were jointly created by several generations. The five-thousand-year-old Chinese *guqin* 古琴 accompanied the development of Chinese civilization, is now a masterpiece in mankind's intangible cultural heritage and a material testimony of Chinese mythology. Emperor Yan tasted a hundred herbs and created the medicine science. The Yellow Emperor started the diagnosis and treatment practice. They respectively contributed greatly to Chinese medicine and medical study. The two ancestors were like doctors, saving the wounded and dying, so they have been deeply respected.

In addition to medicine, the Yellow Emperor also had several other fundamental inventions: firstly, the clothing system. Clothing in the eyes of the Yellow Emperor shows the establishment of social order, just as the saying went, "hands in my sleeves and the world will run as it should 垂衣裳而治天下." Yellow Emperor used clothes as a symbol of orders. This is called "teaching without words." The second invention is cooking with fire, which fundamentally changed people's systems and habits. No wonder China's culinary culture is so developed. The third invention is the vehicle. The Yellow Emperor is also known as "Xuanyuan" 轩辕, which indicates that he was from a cart-making clan. Although it is also said that the chancellor of the Yellow Emperor Xi Zhong 奚仲 was the first to make a vehicle. The fourth invention is the sexagenary cycle, which is extremely important in reckoning time. The fifth, divination and astrology. The sixth is the invention of the writing and drawing by the Yellow Emperor's ministers Cangjie 仓颉 and Shihuang 史皇, respectively. Lastly, he also invented mathematics. The Yellow Emperor and his ministers contributed enormously to the invention of implements and culture, and we can even say they are one of the major creative groups in the world.

Chinese creation mythology emphasizes the creation of cultural systems and scientific invention. This is a very prominent phenomenon. Institutional innovation

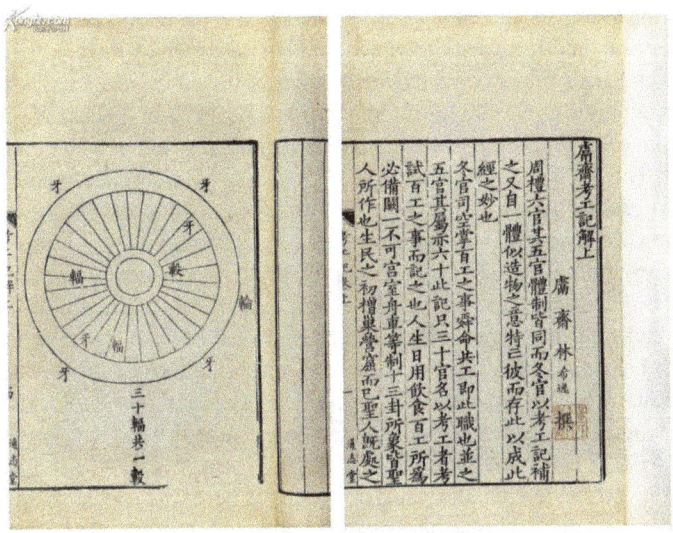

Fig. 2.6 *Book of Diverse Crafts*

is our strength, and scientific and technological innovation is our tradition, so we must carry on this legacy.

In ancient China, the production of utensils was paid close attention and the status of craftsmen was very high. Otherwise, we would not have such a well-developed crafting process of jade, bronze and other artifacts. As a country with advanced craftsmanship, our legends of Qiaochui and Lu Ban, as well as the invention stories of the kings and emperors, greatly elevated craftsmen's status.

In ancient China, there was an important book on inventions and manufacturing, called the *Book of Diverse Crafts* 考工记 (see Fig. 2.6). A classic book that had been constantly improved in the ancient Qin and Han dynasties; it is an encyclopedia of craftsmanship. The book sanctifies the creation of things in the beginning, as it says: "the wise men create things, and the adroit men follow and inherit. They are called craftsmen. 知者创物。巧者述之守之, 世谓之工."

This is the definition of craftsmen, which includes invention and inheritance. Craftsmen are the wise and the adroit—they are elites in the society. Nowadays we sing high praise to craftsmen of some countries to the point of exaggeration. Such willingness to learn and improve is good, but if one belittles our own manufacturing industry as no match to other countries in any aspect that would be excessive humbleness. Some people say that in ancient China, the handicraft industry was despised. This is true in some eras, but Confucian classics did not exclude craftsmen. According to *Book of Diverse Crafts*: "Craftsmen's works are all works of sages 百工之事, 皆圣人之作也."

That is a very high evaluation of craftsman. The craftsmen are sages! How many sages are there? This tradition of Confucian culture was actually resisted by different schools during its development, especially the legalist, who emphasized the significance of peasants and regarded craftsmen and businessmen as lower classes. These views had a negative impact on the development of the Chinese society.

In history, there was a ranking of four occupations: scholars, peasants, craftsmen and businessmen. Agriculture was the most fundamental while industry and business were trivial. This view has long affected the progress of Chinese culture and society. However, *Book of Diverse Crafts* holds another opinion. According to the book: "Those who discuss politics in their seats are called kings and dukes; those who execute orders are called scholar-bureaucrats; those who study shapes and nature of materials and make them into utensils are called craftsmen; those who trade specialties and treasures from different places are called businessmen; those who plow the land to let wealth grow are called peasants; and those who spin and weave to make clothes are working women. 坐而论道, 谓之王公;作而行之, 谓之士大夫;审曲面势, 以饬五材, 以辨民器, 谓之百工;通四方之珍异以资之, 谓之商旅;饬力以长地财, 谓之农夫;治丝麻以成之, 谓之妇功。"

Therefore, you can tell that the status of craftsmen here was very high. In the occupational order of "kings, scholar-bureaucrats, craftsmen, businessmen, peasants, and female textile makers," craftsmen's status was nothing like their low status in the later times. This posed a question: Why were the Confucian classics tampered and were made into a decree that led a paradigm shift in the social hierarchy, while traditional value was marginalized? Along with it, the myths about implement creation were also marginalized.

In Chinese culture, there has always been a balance created by multiple streams of power. In the past, craftsmen and businessmen had been considered lowly. But when I was writing my first book, *A History of Merchants* 商贾史, I surprisingly found that it was Emperor Yan who created the commercial market, a business legend in the mythical era. As to the first businessman, I personally believe it was Emperor Shun, who was not only a god of pottery, but also a commercial practitioner.

When we carefully study China's creation mythology, we will find that the god who created Man is also the god who created things, and even cultures. These gods are also craftsmen and scientists—the creators of all kinds of implements and systems. Chinese creation mythology is profound, and this heritage nourishes the spiritual world of the Chinese.

Chinese creation mythology has been passed down in live forms and is far from becoming outdated like the chrysanthemums after the Double Ninth Festival. This kind of inheritance is manifest in various forms, among which landscape creation and ritual performances are most prominent.

Take the myth of Nüwa for an example, we can see that an ancient story is still full of vitality. The myth of Nüwa has been promoted in many places. For example, under the leadership of the Development and Reform Commission of Xihua, Zhoukou in Henan province, there is a Nüwa forum and a Hall of Creation (see Fig. 2.7).

The Nüwa Palace is even more incredible. People host grand song-and-dance shows there. The photo below is the grand ceremony for the Year of the Sheep. Nüwa became an attraction, and the culture of mythology became a great resource for local economy (see Fig. 2.8).

Fig. 2.7 Local Nüwa forum

Fig. 2.8 Nüwa Palace in She County, Hebei province

As a cultural and economic resource, creation mythology has received more attention than ever before. Various fairs and conferences are being held to promote Nüwa culture. In addition to Hebei province, other provinces such as Gansu also achieved great success in promoting Nüwa culture (see Fig. 2.9).

Nüwa is generally worshiped in the following places:

(1) Chengji County, Longxi, Tianshui city, Gansu province: Nüwa Cave, Nüwa Temple; Hometown of Nüwa at the Dadiwan Ruins
(2) Pingli County, Shaanxi province: hometown of Nüwa, there is a Nüwa Mountain and a Nüwa Temple.

Fig. 2.9 Nüwa Temple in Tianshui, Gansu province

(3) She County, Hebei province: Nüwa Palace
(4) Jincheng County, Zezhou city, Shanxi province: Huaxia Nüwa Cultural Park
(5) Xihua County, Zhoukou city, Henan province: Nüwa City.

In fact, many more events are related to creation mythology. Besides Nüwa, dozens of creation gods have been worshipped in different temples in China on various festivals and fairs. One creation god is often worshipped and commemorated in various places. For example, many places have facilities or festivals to commemorate Yu, such as Beichuan of Sichuan province, Shaoxing of Zhejiang province, Wuhan of Hubei province, Xiaxian of Shanxi province, and Tushan of Anhui province.

The inheritance of creation mythology cannot do without the production and narrative of the landscapes. Through temples, statues and murals, creation mythology is visualized and presented vividly. This is the so-called image narrative. Landscape is also the venue and vehicle to hold ceremonies. The production of landscape and production of ceremonies are synchronized, but the former is the presentation of things and the latter is human behavior. One is static, and one is dynamic. Thus, creation mythology is inherited vividly and lively.

We are grateful for our ancestors' creations. They granted us our lives, created culture and institutions, and invented the production system. All above became the premise and foundation of the development of Chinese culture and cultural enterprises.

Mythology is also the origin of craftsmanship. Tu Youyou testing artemisinin on herself during experiments is a modern version of Shennong tasting hundreds of herbs. An ancient creator can also be mentioned together with Nobel Prize laureates. Hence, creation mythology is tightly tied with craftsmanship. We can understand ourselves and the world through creation mythology. Heaven and Earth nourished all beings, and ancestors produced the human being. Our ancestors created utensils, culture and systems. We should worship the source of our lives and carry on filial piety; worship ancestors' creation and inherit craftsman spirit. Creation mythology is the beginning of our great tradition, and a part of humanism passed down through generations!

Chapter 3
The Flying Dragon and the Dancing Phoenix: Chinese Totem Myths

Shuxian Ye

Professor Shuxian Ye, Zhi Yuan Chair Professor at Shanghai Jiao Tong University and doctoral supervisor at the School of Humanities, successively served as the Director of Comparative Literature Research Center at Chinese Academy of Social Sciences (CASS) and Researcher at CASS Institute of Literature, Vice President of Chinese Folk Literature and Art Association, President of Chinese Mythology Society, Vice President of Chinese Comparative Literature Association, President of Chinese Literary Anthropology Research Society and member of the expert panel of the National Social Science Fund of China.

Before we get into the main content of this chapter, I want to introduce two pairs of concepts: the first pair is literary anthropology and the quadruple evidence method; and the second is the cultural theory of the macro and the micro tradition. In mythology studies, there is a new school of thought that advocates a special type of methodology. This school of thought is called literary anthropology. It differs from traditional methodology in that it does not only study written texts, but also non-textual evidences, particularly archaeological discoveries. This school offers an innovative approach to the study of Chinese totem mythology. It still has certain problems, and at present it is still in the exploratory stage. The special methodology advocated by literary anthropologists is called the "the quadruple evidence method". Here I wish to highlight the idea of dividing cultural traditions into two different levels. One is the macro tradition, which precedes written language and cannot be found in written texts passed down from the past. The other is called the micro tradition, which is the tradition that is recorded in written texts. The knowledge we learn used to be entirely from the micro tradition, whereas the macro tradition had been beyond our imagination. Today, I want to mainly discuss the holy objects in the macro tradition. You can find many books for reference. Here I want to talk about two sets of published books. One is the "Mythology Studies Series 神话学文库" (Shaanxi Normal University General Publishing House Co., Ltd.), which currently contains 38 books, including translations of foreign classics, the latest research findings in Western mythology studies, and the fruits of in-depth research into Chinese mythology from new perspectives. Another is the "Mythistory Series" 神话历史丛书 (Nanfang Daily Press), which currently contains 10 books that consist mainly of investigations into the important ancient Chinese classics from the perspective of Mythistory. The first studied classic is the *Spring and Autumn Annals* 春秋, which chronicles the events of the state of Lu in the Spring and Autumn period. Starting from the first month of the first year under the reign of the Duke Yin of Lu (722 B.C.), the book ends at an event 242 years later: the capture of a *qilin* (unicorn) in a westbound hunt. The *qilin* does not exist in reality, so why does a historical record stop abruptly at the capture of a legendary animal? Obviously, it was supported by the belief that *qilin* existed. Another book in the Mythistory Series is called *Confucian Mythology* 儒家神话. People used to believe that Confucius avoided talking about the unreal and the supernatural, that mythology was only handed down in the Taoist tradition while Confucianism focused only on concrete reality. That is actually a great misunderstanding. Confucius most wanted to dream of a phoenix. What does "the phoenix doesn't arrive" mean? The phoenix was a mythological bird in Confucius' imagination, which proves that the origins of Confucianism are tied in with mythology. This is a fact completely forgotten by modern scholars. So the Mythistory series uses interdisciplinary approaches to re-examine the Chinese classics. Another book is about our nation's neighbor to the east: *Korean Mythistory* 韩国神话历史. This is the thesis written by a Korean PhD student under my supervision in the Chinese Academy of Social Sciences. I think it was an excellent job. From this book you can learn how the Korean people's mythologies were constructed, and how closely related they are with China.

Our starting point is the study of totems. There is a school of literary criticism that was quite popular in the mid 20th century. It studied the mythological archetypes used in literary works. This school is called archetypal mythology criticism, simply referred to as archetypal criticism. Some call it totemic criticism. The book *Mythology: Archetypal Criticism* 神话——原型批评 was written in 1986 and published in 1987, some thirty years ago. The study of myths and totems in China is usually traced back to the early period of Reform and Opening Up under the direction of Deng Xiaoping. At that time there was a new fashion in methodology among scholars in the humanities that introduced to China the various schools of thought prevailing in the West. Mythological archetype criticism was particularly prominent within this movement. The problem that we were trying to solve was how to adapt the schools of Western theoretical criticism to resolving questions within the realm of Chinese scholarship. The year 2011 saw the second edition of the above-mentioned book, twice as large as the first edition. Beginning from theoretical questions, it applied the methodology of archetypal criticism to seeking the origins of images and personages in spetiers of evidencecific literary works. Through thirty years of developing this methodology, combining literary and anthropological research, we proposed the "the quadruple evidence method".

First, I will briefly introduce the quadruple evidence method. The first one is written texts passed down over the ages. Before the Qing dynasty, academic research focused on the study of these classical writings, and Sinology was purely the study of the classics, i.e. the interpretation of the important classical writings, so that the orthodox school of Sinology (national studies) was philology. However, after the so-called oracle bone script was discovered at Anyang in 1899, people realized that the

Chinese script found underground was earlier than that found in the ancient written texts. Later, inscriptions on ancient bronze vessels were discovered; these were all new materials not known before the Qing dynasty. This type of script is referred to as the second tier of evidence, as taught by the great scholar Wang Guowei in his courses at Tsinghua University in 1925. Since then, in studying Chinese culture, scholars have been able to study not only the texts passed down in the tradition, but also this body of information not accessible in the texts. The focus of Wang Guowei's research was oracle bone script, which he used some ninety years ago to solve questions regarding the history of the Shang dynasty. The third tier of evidence is oral tradition and intangible (non-material) cultural heritage. Oral culture consists of ritual chants, dances and recitations transmitted among the populace by elders and religious leaders. An epic that was recently discovered in China, even longer than *The Iliad and The Odyssey* combined, is the oral narrative of an elder of the Miao nationality in Mashan, Guizhou province. In the past, nobody treated this narrative as a subject of study. But a dropout student from Minzu University of China translated it into Han Chinese, drawing the attention of specialists in Chinese folk traditions. Funds were specially allocated to send scholars into the mountains to make a video recording, and the narrative was then published by the Zhonghua Book Company in two grand volumes entitled *Xiud Yax Lus Qim* 亚鲁王 (*King Yalu*). The launching ceremony was held in the Great Hall of the People in Beijing, and it was attended by many government leaders. In ancient times, especially, the area of China that was covered by written script was mainly the central plain from Anyang and Luoyang to the Shaanxi region, while the vast majority of China lay outside of the realm of written script. Thus, in studying Chinese culture, we cannot rely only on the information transmitted through written texts. We have to step out of the prison of written script and utilize three the quadruple evidence method, which is significant in expanding the horizon of cultural studies. In the past oral history was only taught in universities that had professors specializing in folk literature. If a university didn't have this track, no one would teach oral culture. That is a real shame. Some scholars, as researchers in anthropology, took the study of aboriginal peoples as their main field of research. 99% of these peoples have no writing at all. So how did they conduct research? First, through oral culture. Second, by relying on writing ethnological studies based on field investigations into the lifestyle of people in villages or tribes. There are also implements used in daily life, and this constitutes the fourth tier of evidence, which is borrowed from anthropology. The fourth tier of evidence that we discuss here refers specifically to cultural artifacts and images, which we know about from archaeological excavations and field studies. Archeology is a branch of anthropology that studies cultural artifacts. We don't know if our ancestors could tell stories from the artifacts, as there was no writing. Today, telling history through cultural artifacts is a new fashion, and it is an important avenue for updating our historical records. Since 2005 I have attempted to combine the above-mentioned four aspects, naming them the quadruple evidence method. In this there is an upgrade of thought and knowledge. In the past, all discussions of Chinese things were based upon written texts. Now with this the quadruple evidence method, we have greatly expanded our horizon and deepened our understanding of history.

Fig. 3.1 Dragon-and-Phoenix Jade Pendant, Hongshan Culture, unearthed in Niuheliang, Liaoning. Dated to ca. 5000 years ago

This picture shows something unearthed in the 21st century. Archaeologists and professional collectors would recognize this object with just one glance that it depicts a dragon and a phoenix (see Fig. 3.1). This jade approximately 5,000 years old was unearthed in Jianping County, Liaoning province, where archaeologists found the most prehistoric jade objects that belonged to the Hongshan Culture. But people had never seen a dragon and a phoenix carved together on one jade object. Is this a dragon and a phoenix combined in one body? Scholars have not agreed on this but based on the image archaeologists have named it the "Dragon-and-Phoenix Jade Pendant." More research is needed in order to know what exactly it depicts. At least it shows that myths and totems were produced and used in the region of ancient Chinese culture thousands of years before the oracle bone script. As our research methodology and knowledge reach a higher level, we no longer rely solely on the limited information contained in written texts to research the prehistoric totem.

Cultural traditions can be distinguished into two stages: one with written language and one without. The library, as the treasure house and palace of knowledge, brings together all of the written materials. In the past, when archeology wasn't developed, we didn't know how big and fantastic the world beyond words really is. *A Study of Cultural Symbols: New Perspectives on the Macro and Micro Tradition* 文化符号学——大小传统新视野, published in 2013, is one book in the Mythology Studies series. This book is about the theories and methodologies in the research of macro and micro tradition. What is the micro tradition? The tradition found in written records since the oracle bone scripts and bronze inscriptions appeared is called the micro tradition. Anthropologists have discovered that over 90% of ethnic groups in the world have no written language. We can't assume that the written language used by a minority of people contain the whole of mankind's knowledge. Therefore, anthropologists pay special attention to the unwritten cultural tradition. People who have no written language can all be said to live in the macro tradition. In terms of space, the macro tradition is not far from us. The Miao elder in Mashan whom I mentioned earlier can recite over 10,000 lines of the epic. The macro tradition originates from the oral culture era and lasts till today without interruption. But we scholars pay too much attention on the written tradition and look down on the unwritten culture tradition. The concepts of the macro and micro traditions shook our perspective on knowledge. The macro tradition exists before the written language, and it uses objects like paintings and sculptures to convey information. Art came into being before the written language. The macro tradition comes into being earlier than written language, and the space that it covers is much greater. Through the dichotomy of medium, this is a new theoretical framework provided by cultural semiotics for our search for totems. All of the micro tradition and everything found in written records were derived from the macro tradition. Take the Chinese characters for example, which are the pictographic characters used by the Chinese. In the early stage, every Chinese character was an image. It was very easy to find its archetype, which is the physical object represented by the image. By tracing the physical objects, we found some key totems of the Han Chinese.

The two books mentioned before are on theories. *Mythology: Archetypal Criticism* is on the theories and methodologies of totem criticism. What is a totem? Simply put, first, it is a holy object for worship. Second, it originated from the consanguinity of a clan. For example, some think that our ancestors were derived from the dragon and the phoenix, but only when the dragon and the phoenix meet the above two conditions, they can be called totems. We believe that the dragon and the phoenix come into being at a later time. What existed before them are two real-world animals called *Chixiao*, or the owl, and the bear. So we conclude: the phoenix and the dragon were transformed from the owl and the bear. This conclusion might be shocking to someone. Let me analyze it for you.

People are familiar with the concept of "dragon's descendants", but that is a modern phrase. In ancient China, the dragon has undergone two phases divided by the Qin dynasty. What did the dragon look like before the Qin dynasty? What did it look like after? Now let's get into the change of the dragon. Let me introduce my third book: *An Illustrated History of the Origin of Chinese Civilization* 图说中华文明发生史, published in 2015. It accounts how the Chinese culture came into being through mythological totems over 8,000 years ago until the West Zhou dynasty. That was the period when the Han Chinese culture was formed. People knew very well what happened after that. That book used two chapters to discuss how the phoenix and the dragon were transformed from the owl and the bear: one chapter on the prototype of dragons, and the other on the prototype of phoenix. Please take a look at the cover of the book first (Fig. 3.2), which is an example from the fourth tier of

Fig. 3.2 *An illustrated history of the origin of Chinese civilization*

evidence, which is a piece of jade relic. A glance, you'll know what it is. After the dragon, let's talk about the relationship between dragon and human. Please note, we are not talking about "the dragon's descendants". In the dragon-human relationship, the dragon is gigantic, and the human is very small. In fact, the dragon is humans' vehicle that can freely access the sky, the earth and the sea. This newly unearthed relic from Jingzhou, Hubei, shows a person standing on the dragon's tail to go up to the heaven from the ground. Where was it unearthed? Xiongjia Zhong (the Xiong Family Tomb), as known by locals. This jade pendant tells us that since the pre-Qin era, dragon had been a supernatural vehicle. If you don't believe it, just take a look at *the Book of Change*.

The dragon dive deep into the water or soar into the sky. It is unrelated to the ancestors, totem or descendants. At least during the Spring and Autumn era, many interpretations about the dragon have appeared. You will understand what "flying dragon in the sky" is instantly. In totem mythology, the most representative motifs are dragon and phoenix, which are two subjects that are the most familiar to the Chinese people. Modern scholars have written many works on the dragon and phoenix. You can read them on your own. My point is, totem mythology is very important. It originates in the prehistoric society. "Totem" comes from the language of American

3 The Flying Dragon and the Dancing Phoenix: Chinese Totem Myths

Fig. 3.3 Collection of the Han stone reliefs in Xiao County, Anhui, 2013

Indians. They don't have the written language. At the door of each clan placed a holy object or a wooden sculpture, or in other forms. That is totem, which mostly are animals from the real life. That is the original meaning of totem in the American Indian culture. Anthropologists expanded the meaning of this word. As a result, Chinese dragon and phoenix are labeled as totems. But the totem in American Indian culture copy from the real animals, such as the crow or the frog. In China, things are opposite. The dragon, phoenix and *qilin* that the Chinese talk about are nowhere to be found in reality. They are imaginations from religion and mythology. The question is, how are they imagined? Why those animals? Once you understand the totem mythology, you open the door to the Chinese culture. Without such understanding, you can only read the works by modern scholars without touching the heart of the Chinese culture. In fact, the Chinese culture has been constructed on mythological imagination since the Xia, Shang and Zhou dynasties.

This picture is a typical example (Fig. 3.3). I always assign it as homework to my new graduate students and let them recognize how many images are in the picture. People with knowledge about the Han dynasty probably know what this picture is for. The stone reliefs from the Han dynasty are for the dead people's use. They depict the next life in his tomb. The Chinese people firmly believe that death is not the end of one's life. There must be an afterlife. So they respect the dead as much as the living, and buried the most valuable things in the grave, as many new discoveries from the ancient tombs. In the Han dynasty, if the dead were nobler than the aristocrats, people would dedicate a stone relief to him. On one side is a circle with a three-legged crow in the middle. That is the sun. The Chinese people believe that a three-legged bird is in the middle of the sun, or the sun is on the back of this bird. On the other side is the moon. The circle is the moon with a rabbit and a toad in the middle. People who are familiar with the cultural motifs know that it is the moon. People from other countries or ethnic groups might not understand it if they are not familiar with the Han Chinese culture. The sun and the moon on each side define the sky, the universe, the transformation between yin and yang, light and darkness, and life and death. That points out the direction for the soul of the dead. Often, we can find such image on the lintel of the Han stone relief. If you are familiar with Daoism, you can recognize that on the left is the Azure Dragon (*Qinglong*), and the right, the White Tiger (*Baihu*). The dragon symbolizes the East, and the tiger, the West. Though absent with two other animals, the dragon and the tiger have already outlined the typical square universe in the Chinese mind. The other two are the Black Tortoise (*Xuanwu*) and the Vermilion Bird (*Zhuque*). There is a Xuanwu Gate in Nanjing, and a Zhuque Gate in Xi'an. Both are from the Chinese people's imagination and mythology. The four directions are represented by the four animals. Anywhere they appear, you will know there is a universe. We haven't talked about the most important thing: what stands in the middle of the Azure Dragon and the White Tiger? We know that in Chinese, China literally means the middle kingdom. The most powerful country in the whole universe must be in the middle.

So, the central position is for the holiest of all, which is the king of gods in the universe. What is that? It looks like a *qilin*, a two-footed animal dancing, which has a little tail too. You might be able to tell, that it is a holy bear standing in the central position in the sky. Don't equate it as the bears in the zoo. I once watched the TV show *Chinese Martial Arts*. One of the moves is called "the bear sway," which is from the legendary physician Hua Tuo's Wuqinxi (the Exercise of Five Animals). Many moves in Chinese martial art are copied from animals, as people think those animals are strong and energetic, and hope that they can be as strong through imitating their moves. Though we don't know exactly how it works, the moves are kept till today. That shows the power of the third layer of evidence. In Hua Tuo's time, the bear was god. Imitating its moves is a way of exercising our spirit. This picture is from the fourth source of evidence, which is more effective than any text. When an ancient image is unearthed, as long as it is not a forgery, it represents that era's views of the world and the universe. Both the Azure Dragon and the White Tiger are strong animals. Why are they just sidekicks of the bear? We need to look for the reason from the transformation of the owl and the bear into phoenix and dragon.

As animal totem appeared, plant totem came into being too. Let's look at two words, one is *sheji* (社稷, grain, state), and the other is *jingshen* (精神, rice, spirit). From the shape of these characters, we can tell that the first character of the first word, *she* 社 is related to the earth, from which crops grow. The second character, *ji* 稷, makes us think of a piece in the *Book of Poetry* on the ancestors of the Zhou people. Their ancestors are called "ji." *Ji* literally means the millets, a type of staple food. Before the flour and wheat were imported around 4,000 years ago, people in Northern China mainly ate the millet. So the earliest millet we found dates back to 8,000 years ago. Ji, as totem and the name of the Zhou people's ancestors, means staple food. *Sheji*: It means what grew from the yin-natured earth by planting the yang-natured seed. In the past, people thought the most important thing was the food that supported their survival. The rice grows in South China, so *jingshen* was created by people in the South. *Jing* means rice. Zhuangzi was the first to use the word "jingshen." He lived in the Huai River region in Anhui, which produced a lot of rice. "Jing" and "ji" are the essence of crops, whose growth is propelled by the endless circle of life, as we see the spring sowing and fall harvesting. Behind these two characters lie the prototypes of ancient Chinese civilization. Through the characters, we found the physical objects they refer to. Both are the essence of crops.

As a nation of agriculture, people consider crops as sacred. Next two books are about *sheji* and *jingshen*. The first book, published in 1997, examined the concept of *sheji*. It was called *The High-Tang Goddess and Venus* 高唐神女与维纳斯. The second one, *A Cultural Interpretation of Zhuangzi* 庄子的文化解析, discussed "Jingshen" and the origin of the concept of "jing," or essence, in Sect. 5, Chap. 11. You will understand why "jing" (white rice) is followed by "shen" (god) in the word "jingshen" (spirit). For over 10,000 years, the Chinese people have been relying on the rice as staple food. In Jiangxi and Hunan, carbonized rice has been unearthed, which is over 10,000 years old. Our habit of eating rice provides the best clue in the study of totem, because that's where the Chinese characters come from. This is what literary anthropologists said, texts are micro tradition. If you do research only through written texts, you can only go as far back as the appearance of written words. Only by looking back before the invention of written texts can we really learn what was worshiped in the macro tradition, which is as wide as the sea.

What is the relationship between the plant totem and the animal totem? Anthropologists explained that people started farming around 10,000 years ago. Before that, nobody planted or ate crops. Instead, they ate the prey, as everyone was a hunter in the Hunting Era, which existed before the agricultural society. Non-animal food was something to be gathered, such as the wild berries. It was a hunter-gatherer era. Nobody farmed. You worshiped the animals that you lived on. We consider the totem of the hunting and gathering culture came earlier than that in the agricultural societies. If humans were evolved from the great apes, then they lived on hunting over three million years ago. Just imagine, over 10,000 years ago when there were no crops on earth, what did people imagine or worship? It must have been animals. The ears of the crops are compared to their heads. Only by cutting off their heads can people eat their grains. Sowing in the spring is a festive event, but when fall arrives, things become solemn. People never simply eat their harvest without rituals to worship the crops. So the odes in the *Book of Songs* are mostly about repayment to the land in the fall. In the past, the stage plays were called "shexi" (the earth play). Those were not for the general public, but for the god of the earth. The purpose was to thank the earth's blessings. Before the Qing dynasty, putting on a play was considered sacred. Now we understand the sacred conducts performed for the land and crops. Moreover, people consider there is telepathy between the heads of crops and the heads of people. That is reflected in the head-hunting witchcraft in the prehistoric agricultural societies. At the Chinese border in Yunnan province live a people called the *Wa* people. A survey in the 1950s revealed that villagers put human heads at their doors. Obviously head hunting was still a popular practice then. Not long ago, a film *Warriors of the Rainbow: Seediq Bale* directed by Wei Te-sheng was aired. The show started with head hunting. The tribe only hunts men's heads. After the hunting, they blend the brain and blood with the soil, and spread on the land of the whole tribe in the spring. It is a pray for harvest using the human head's vitality to boost the growth of crops' heads (the seeds). That is the earliest belief of the agricultural society. The core idea comes from the hunting era, that the vitality is stored in the head. This belief is often reflected in folk painting. The god of longevity is represented by a large head, but nobody could explain the reason. People in the agricultural era firmly believed that the head was the source of vigor and vitality. In traditional Chinese medicine, the theory of life is summarized in these few words: replenish essence to nourish the brain. People used to believe that the essence is stored in the head. The agricultural ideology was centered on crops, human heads, and crop heads. It originated from the beliefs about animal heads in the hunting era. From the hunting era to the agricultural society, mythologies changed, but a belief remained consistent. That is: vitality comes from a sacred source.

Where can we find a physical evidence of the bear totem? In the 1980s, the once obscure place Niuheliang in Jianping County of Liaoning province suddenly became well-known all over the world. The Liaoning government built a museum with RMB ¥500 million of investment, and called it "the world's biggest museum on prehistoric sites."

A temple of over 5,000 years was discovered there. People call it "The First Temple in China" or "The First Temple in East Asia". People usually associate temples with Buddhism, but in prehistoric era, to worship the earth, erecting a pole is enough. To one's surprise, this place has a temple with idols: the bear sculpture and a real bear skull with only the jawbone. The upper part is missing (see Fig. 3.4). Zoologists

Fig. 3.4 A bear skull found in the Goddess Temple, Niuheliang, Liaoning province, dated ca. 6,000 years ago

Fig. 3.5 A bear skull found in a human cave site of the Paleolithic age in Jinniushan, Liaoning, dated ca. 280,000 years ago

would know instantly that it is a bear. Why is a bear skull placed in a temple of over five or six thousand years ago?

An even earlier discovery was made in a human cave site of the same age in Jinniushan, Liaoning. People of that time mainly ate the prey. Researchers found a gigantic bear skeleton in the cave with the skull in a prominent place (see Fig. 3.5).

Currently the skull is preserved in the Arthur M. Sackler Museum of Art and Archeology at Peking University. While it is a small museum, its collections are of great importance. 280,000 years ago, people's food was mainly animals. People ate bears too. Some peoples roaming in the Stanovoy Range region still keeps their hunting traditions. They didn't develop the written language. We translated their oral accounts, which were all about the bear totem. They call bears "grandpa and grandma," and believe that the origin of life lies in animals, which is the same as Korean culture. In Korea, the most popular stage play nowadays is about the worship of the bear mother. They think that their first king, Dangun, was the son of a bear. We thought we were descendants of the dragon, but we forgot that the bear had been active in the Chinese history for over 10,000 years. Why is the Goddess Temple in Niuheliang so valuable? Because it is the only complete religious structure of five thousand years old found in China. It has an idol inside, and its history dates back thousands of years earlier than the oracle bone script.

That is an example from the fourth source of evidence, the evidence for the macro tradition culture. Why is it called a Goddess Temple? Because one fragment of the

Fig. 3.6 A clay bear head and a paw of 5,000 years ago, unearthed in the Goddess Temple in Niuheliang

shattered statues, mostly made of clay, was obviously women's breast, anthropologists thus named it as Goddess Temple. Along with the goddess statue were two kinds of animals: birds of prey and beast of prey. Both the real bear skull and the clay bear head and paw were found in the Goddess Temple. The teeth were colored with white lime. The paw is undoubtedly a bear paw as it is so wide and fat (see Fig. 3.6).

In the Han stone relief discussed before, the central position of the universe is occupied by a bear. You might wonder, why not a tiger? Yes, tigers are fierce, but back in prehistoric era, bears were the most powerful. *Rites of Zhou* 周礼 recorded that "on the flag is a bear and a tiger." In the prehistoric age, the bear came before the tiger. There are stories behind the holy bear. What is the other name of the Yellow Emperor? Youxiong (Bear Present). You know about the TV show *The Legend of*

Mi Yue. Mi was a major family name in Chu, but after the Chu king became emperor, his families changed their last name to Xiong (bear). The great historian Sima Qian recorded 25 Chu kings named after Xiong. Nobody asked why. Is there anything to doubt about bears appearing in a 5,000-year-old temple? This temple alone can prove that the early people in East Asia worshiped bears in the temple. That is indeed a groundbreaking discovery. We have the quadruple evidence method: the real bear and the bear sculpture. Why were bears worshiped? It is very simple. Write down the character "bear (熊)." Just using one second to make a connection, you will understand. Delete the four dots (paws) underneath, we have the original form of the character: 能 (able). The four dots (paws) were added to differentiate a physical being from an abstract concept that is related to ability (能力) and energy (能源). Then we knew: bears are able. Why? Bears' hibernation lasts for five or six months, during which they seem dead, but they come out alive in summer. That is the life energy of rejuvenation. Without external force, one comes back to life. No creature is more able than that. People want to have this ability, so they added bear-like movements in martial arts practice. Before going into hibernation, bears eat whatever it can find and double their weight. They survive on the energy stored in their body for the next five winter months. In North China, a practice is to "put on autumn fat." That is bionics. In 2005, the National Museum of China held an exhibition of the intangible heritage of all peoples in China. All ethnic groups brought their treasures, which were held secret within the clan.

Nanai people from Northern China took out their bear totem sowed on fish skin, which had been treasured for generations (see Fig. 3.7). The bear totem is not far from us at all. Briar and Bramble from the animation *Boonie Bears* didn't contain any cultural connotation. If the director could learn more about the source of Chinese totem, things will be different.

Bear Totem: An Exploration of the Ancestor Myths of the Han Chinese 熊图腾:中华祖先神话探源, was inspired by a 2004 best-seller novel, *The Wolf Totem* 狼图腾, which was adapted into a film by a French director and shown during the Spring Festival holiday in 2015. But the film wasn't as well-received as the novel. We cannot but face the reality when studying Chinese totem. The first half of *The Wolf Totem* are stories, and the second half are dialogues and discussions on whether the Chinese people are descendants of the dragon or the wolf. The author thinks that the dragon was transformed from the wolf. After *The Wolf Totem*, many people followed suits and published wolf-related books. Some business leaders advocated that only through teamwork, like the wolf pack, could strong competitiveness be generated. The dragon is outdated. Time to change it to the wolf. We researchers must figure out if the wolf is the Chinese totem. The discussion in the second half of Wolf Totem thinks that the dragon was transformed form the wolf. As stated previously, two conditions must be met before something becomes the totem: one is a worshiped idol, and the other is blood relation. Historically, some nations indeed worshipped the wolf. Ancient Rome was one of them. Because the founders of the Roman Empire, twin brothers Romulus and Remus, were raised by a wolf, the Romans worshiped wolves. Is there any evidence to prove that the wolf is the totem in China? Can anyone find out evidence? Just take a look at the set phrases that are related to the

Fig. 3.7 The bear totem on fish skin, Nanai people

wolf: *lang zi ye xin* (wolf child's ambition, a derogatory expression for one's evil ambitions) and *lang xin gou fei* (wolf heart and dog lung, a derogatory expression for an ungrateful person), which had nothing to do with totem. Therefore, the notion of wolf totem is basically groundless. If we apply the quadruple evidence method, the conclusion would be that instead of the wolf, the totem is the bear. We need evidence to win a case. If you were a judge, how would you judge? You would need to apply the quadruple evidence method.

The sacred objects related to the bear, as unearthed in China, are the bear skulls and bear sculptures of thousands of years ago. Internationally, the earliest object dates back to 30,000 years ago. Archaeologists discovered Chauvet Cave in Southern France that used to belong to hunters in the Paleolithic Age. Inside the cave, a bear skull was placed on the alter. At the entrance of the cave are two color-painted bears, one big and one small (see Fig. 3.8). If you don't understand it, I recommend a book titled *A Cultural Discovery in the Classic of Mountains and Seas*. That is one of the ten books that we will focus on. *The Classic of Mountains and Seas* tells of a mountain called the Bear Mountain with a cave called the Bear Cave. In fact, that

Fig. 3.8 The earliest oil painting in Chauvet Cave, dated 30,000 years ago

best explains the picture we discussed. Though they are not in the same place, the mythological imagination is essentially the same. What's special about the Bear Cave is that it closes in winter and opens in summer. Also, as the book tells, "gods always emerge from there." Take a look at the Bear Mountain and the Bear Cave: it closes at winter, as if the source of life takes a break. In summer, the bears come out. The picture of 30,000 years ago is at the entrance of Chauvet Cave in France. It shows the awaken bear after hibernation, which symbolizes revival. To people in the past, there are only spring and fall. Spring includes summer, and fall includes winter. People of the Hunting Age treated their prey as symbols of the circle of life. We call the picture the earliest oil painting, which is colored.

We know that the mythology of the Bear Mountain and the Bear Cave is that the bear is worshiped on the alter. The Japanese archipelago is home to the Ainu people, which has a longer history than the Yamato people. The Ainu people set on the Japanese archipelago approximately 20,000 years ago, and they lived on bear-hunting. The bear represents the heavenly god. Every bear in reality is considered the appearance of a god. The bear and the god are the same. People eat the bear's meat, but worship its skull, so that its soul can return to the heaven, and turn into a bear next year to provide food for the Ainu. We saw this pattern in the Ainu people on the Japanese archipelago. The prey worship in the hunting age is special because of what was worshiped. The bear is one of the fierce animals on land. Though the tiger is equally fierce, it is smaller than the bear and it doesn't go into hibernation, which doesn't trigger the association with energy.

Some people don't believe the bear worship. But please take a look at the third layer of evidence: a ritual performer puts on the bearskin to represent the descending of the heavenly god (Fig. 3.9). That is the Shaman Dance to God. The god's spirit is on the Shaman. This totem mythology is still performed today, which is called intangible

Fig. 3.9 The heavenly bear mythology: Heavenly god descends to be Shaman

heritage. It has captured all our imagination about the bear. If you understand it, you will know that the godly bear is not just an imagination.

Is there more evidence to prove that the bear was the major god in heaven in the hunting age? Our evidence is all from the prehistoric jade ware. Jade itself is a Chinese totem. It is inorganic, but it is treated as a totem, just as the jade pendant of Jia Baoyu in the literary classic Dream of the Red Chamber. Jade represents the heaven, god and everlasting life. It is more important than life. A museum in Niuheliang was built to display the jade objects unearthed there. Please take a look at this jade three-hole bridge (Fig. 3.10). This bridge is not a regular one, but a rainbow bridge that connects the earth and the heaven. At the two sides are two human heads, representing the descending of gods. People can hold up this object by putting poles through the three holes, and carry it as an idol. Liaoning Provincial Museum houses the only one "three-hole object with two bear heads" (see Fig. 3.11). It is more than

3 The Flying Dragon and the Dancing Phoenix: Chinese Totem Myths

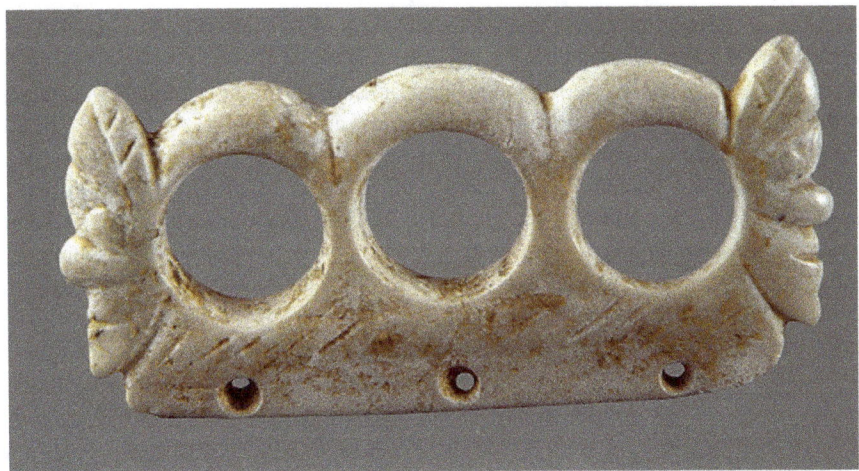

Fig. 3.10 Three-hole object with two human heads, Hongshan culture, dated over 5,000 years ago

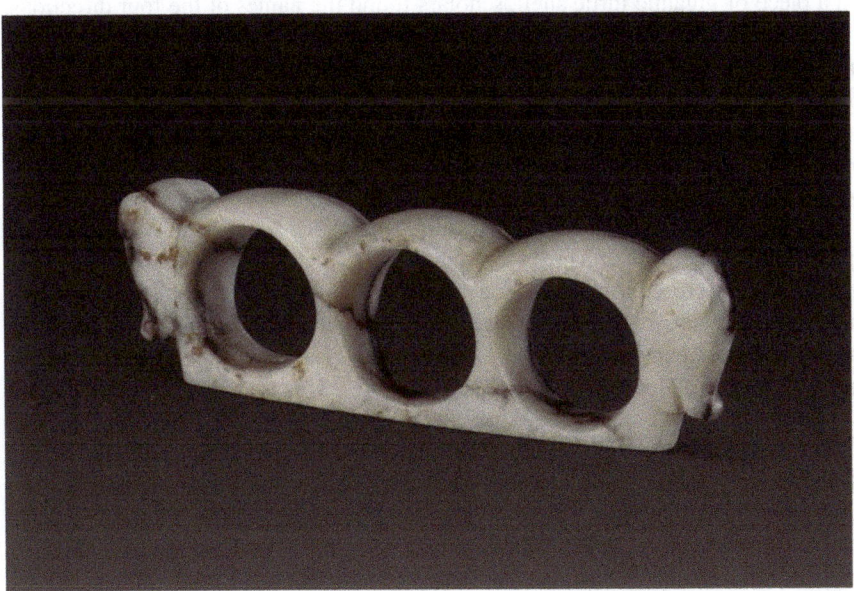

Fig. 3.11 Three-hole jade with two bear heads, Hongshan culture, dated over 5,000 years ago

5,000 years old, and vividly represents people's imagination then. By cutting and carving, people turned jade into sacred object. Not toys, nor daily objects. Harder than glass, jade was very difficult to process. One needed patience and devotion to carve and polish. Every object leads people to the era it belongs to. Jade culture is a process of making materials sacred, as jade was sculptured into sacred objects, idols and religious apparatus. Before the 1980s and the 1990s, nobody had researched or even seen those objects, as they were unearthed recently. By these newly unearthed sacred objects, we discovered the clues and outlines of the holy objects that were used in the early totem worship and found the lost archetypes.

We have talked a lot about how the bear turned into a dragon. So then how did the owl turn into a phoenix? Let's look at the first tier of evidence: written texts passed down in the tradition. The character *feng* in *fenghuang* (phoenix) is very similar to the character *feng* for wind, and they can be understood as a phonetic loan pair. In oracle bone script, the earliest form of the Chinese characters, the two characters are interchangeable. In this way, we can recover the imagination behind the mythology. *The Book of Songs* is divided into three parts: 风 (*feng*), 雅 (*ya*) and 颂 (*song*—ballads, hymns and odes). 风 *feng* is considered to be the largest in quantity and the most expansive in geographical scope. Chapter 8 of *The Book of Songs: A Cultural Hermeneutics* devotes 50,000 characters to the mythology around 风 (*feng*, ballads) and 风 (*feng*, phoenix) and to tracing the origins of these themes in Chinese mythology. Simply put, before 1899, it was an unsolvable puzzle. It wasn't until the discovery of the oracle bone script in 1899 that solving the puzzle became possible. On a piece of gigantic turtle shell, scholars found the names of the four directions. The prognosticators in the Shang dynasty named the gods in the east, west, north and south and equipped them with a phoenix. The eight names were carved on the turtle shell. Our ancient ancestors believed that the winds from all directions were produced by the wings of a great bird (the phoenix) as it takes off. You might find such imagination to be too outlandish. What kind of bird can produce a tornado? But just take a look at the beginning of the chapter 逍遥游 (*Xiaoyaoyou*, A Happy Excursion) of the *Zhuangzi*: "the Bird gathers the force from the tornado and soars up 90,000 *li* (one $li = 500$ m)". No matter what wind it is, even a tornado or a whirlwind, the great bird can produce it without difficulty. Our ancestors thought that the earth is square and that on each side there stands a phoenix. Understanding the ancient interchangeability of 风 (*feng*) and 风 (*feng*) led us to the discovery of the mythological associations of the word 风 (*feng*). This is a micro tradition that we can date back to the oracle bone script era.

Above the micro tradition is the macro tradition: the phoenix found in the design of prehistoric utensils that dated back to 1,000 years earlier than the oracle bone script (see Fig. 3.12). This prehistoric phoenix is characterized by a long and curled tail with a crown on its head. This is a prehistoric utensil in the shape of a phoenix, which was unearthed in Tianmen, Hubei province. It belongs to the Shijiahe culture that is 4,300 years old. It is 1,000 years earlier than the oracle bone script and is part of the macro tradition. The idea found in the oracle bone script that the great wind comes from the flapping of the phoenix's wings must have a historical origin.

But speaking of the earlier and more popular divine bird before the phoenix, it would be the owl. The wide-faced and round-eyed owl. The Western civilization starts at Athens, Greece, whose patron is Athena, the goddess of wisdom. Athena is accompanied by an owl. The owl is a nocturnal bird. Its eyes represent the wisdom that breaks the darkness. Under the pyramid, in the royal tombs of the Pharaoh, symbols that represent the transformation between life and death can be found, which is

Fig. 3.12 Phoenix in the design of a prehistoric utensil, dated 4,300 years ago in Shijiahe culture, Tianmen, Hubei province

guarded by the holy owl. It is said that the Chinese think that the owl bears ill omen, because its squeaks calls disaster. It can communicate with the underworld and takes people's spirit away on behalf of the King of Hell. As a result, nobody thinks the owl is holy today. But if we take a look at the unearthed utensils that belong to the macro tradition, we can find that the most common birds are the hawks and the owls. In the daytime, the birds of prey are eagles and hawks, and in the nighttime, they are the owls.

How have we found that the phoenix and the owl are connected? We have to discover the process of the change of forms, which overall means to find the worshipped object before the phoenix. *The Goddess with a Thousand Faces* 千面女神, published in 2004, devoted one chapter to the worship of the owl image. As to the objects of worship before the written texts, there is still controversy over the appearance of the bear.

But the clay owl face unearthed in Hua County, Shaanxi is undoubtedly the head of an owl. Round face, round eyes. It is dated to around 6,000 years ago (see Fig. 3.13) and belongs to the Yangshao culture. The Yangshao culture was discovered in 1921 in Yangshao village, Mianchi County, Henan. Beginning some 7,000 years ago and ending some 5,000 years ago, this culture lasted nearly 2,000 years. What does it mean? From the first emperor of Qin to the end of the Qing dynasty, the whole feudal society lasted only some 2,000 years. You can tell how long-lived was the Yangshao culture. In that culture earthenware animal sculptures were all considered sacred.

From 6,000 years ago to 5,000 years ago, a culture focused on jade carvings existed in northern China. Jade is the more valuable material, so that objects carved from jade were considered sacred. The turquoise owl of the Hongshan culture, unearthed in Dongshanzui, Kazuo County, Liaoning province has outstretched wings and two protrusions on its head, which are the owl's horn-like feather ruffs (see Fig. 3.14).

Fig. 3.13 A clay owl face unearthed in Hua County, Shaanxi, dating to approximately 6,000 years ago

Among the jade implements from the Hongshan culture unearthed in Liaoning, the hooked cloud jade pendant has aroused controversy. It can be seen as a cloud with curved hooks on both sides. But if one examines the pendant one sees that its most prominent feature is the swirl-shaped round eyes. Only one bird of prey has this sort of eyes, and that is the owl. This pendant actually depicts an owl spreading its wings to fly. The National Palace Museum in Taipei also has a similar object on display, called the beast face with teeth pattern jade pendant (see Fig. 3.15). Beneath the jade pendant are several protrusions. Some scholars think they are the animal's teeth. I think they are actually the tail feathers that open up after the owl spreads its wings. After seeing the "owl god spreading wings" (see Fig. 3.16), we know that the owl worship in the Hongshan culture manifested in several ways: a realistic form, an abstract form and a three-dimensional image expressed in two-dimensional space. To differentiate among them, we mainly rely on the owl's eyes. A number of similar objects have been unearthed, and the differences among them are not great. This indicates that all of the tribal leaders, including those holding political power as well as shamans, all wore similar pendants during ritual ceremonies.

The owl worship lasted without stop from the prehistoric age into the age of written texts, i.e. the micro tradition, but it was cut off during the revolutionary period between the Shang and Zhou dynasties. When one dynasty overthrew the previous one, it had to knock over the previous dynasty's tradition of sacred objects.

3 The Flying Dragon and the Dancing Phoenix: Chinese Totem Myths

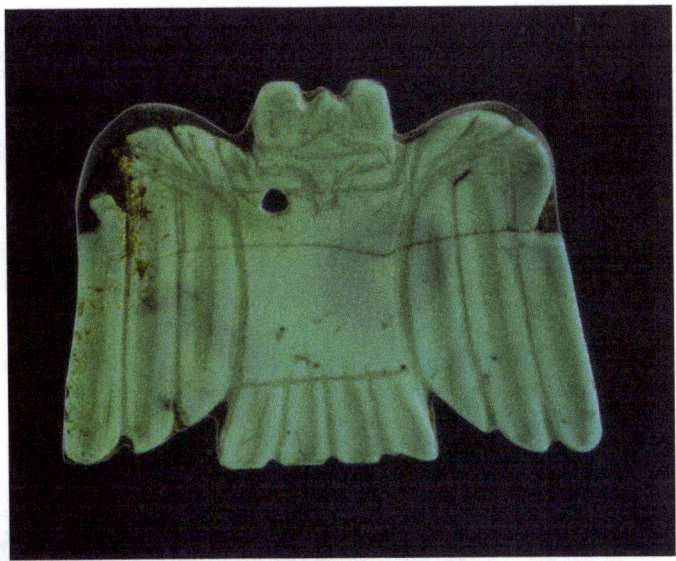

Fig. 3.14 A turquoise owl of the Hongshan culture, unearthed in Dongshanzui, Kazuo, Liaoning, dated 5,000 to 6,000 years ago

Fig. 3.15 "The beast face with teeth pattern jade pendant," named by the National Palace Museum in Taipei

The owl was worshiped both before and during the Shang dynasty. This can best be demonstrated by the high-level tombs of the Shang dynasty. After the 1970s, several astonishing discoveries in some newly excavated tombs revealed something quite different. Several decades ago, Anyang saw the discovery of a number of Shang dynasty tombs, and the most exquisite objects are mostly found now in the collection

Fig. 3.16 The owl god spreading wings: the hooked cloud jade pendant of the Hongshan culture, unearthed in Niuheliang, Liaoning province

Fig. 3.17 The marble owl unearthed from the Yin Ruins Great Tomb 1001 from Academia Sinica in Taipei

of Academia Sinica Museum in Taipei. One of the items was from the Great Tomb 1001. The Great Tomb 1001 is the most high-level tomb that we can now examine. We believe it is the tomb of a Shang dynasty king. None of the animals inside can be a toy or doll; rather they are totems believed in by the Shang people. The Shang dynasty's totem, as recorded in the Book of Songs, is the *xuan* bird (玄鸟, the black bird). What bird is the *xuan* bird? Ancient annotators unanimously agreed that it is the swallow, because *"xuan"* can have the meaning of "black," and the black bird is the swallow. The Shang people believed that their ancestors were born from the swallow, and a state in the Shang dynasty, the Yan state, actually named itself after the swallow (*yanzi*). Did they take the swallow as their totem? We cannot believe the interpretations of the Confucian scholars of the Han dynasty, because the Han flourished approximately 2,000 years ago, and the Shang flourished over 3,000 years ago. The 1,000 years difference makes it necessary to find proof for a lot of aspects of the Shang culture. The best artworks unearthed from the highest-level tomb, Great Tomb 1001, are mostly owl sculptures. The marble owl is one of them (see Fig. 3.17). Carved in marble, it is a rather large sculpture. Its majestic form is totally different from the "night cat" image of the owl that has prevailed in later times. It calls forth associations with the sacred. Its body is covered by carved patterns and its legs are thicker than the legs of a bear. Sitting upright and proper like a king, the owl is called the horned owl, as it has two horn-shaped feather ruffs on its head. It is not enough just to appreciate this sculpture from an artistic perspective. We need to further ask: what is the significance of making this sculpture for the Shang king's tomb? Can it be totally unconnected to the owl worship in Northern China of 6,000 years ago? That is our question.

Outside of marble carvings, one finds many smaller owls carved from jade. The most elegant bronze piece is the owl sculpture found in the Tomb of Fu Hao (see Fig. 3.18). In 1976, archaeologists opened a tomb that had never been broken into. Inside they found over 1,000 bronze and jade carvings. The most exquisite bronzes are a pair of owl sculptures. Now we can see immediately what the sacred bird that the Shang people worshiped was. No swallow sculptures were found in the tomb, so there is no proof that the *xuan* bird is the swallow. This owl sculpture has a very distinct shape. Its form is like an owl with two smaller owls on its head. The wings are curled snake reliefs and the tail is an owl tail, which is used to represent the owl as the revival of the life's energy. The owl is a nocturnal animal, and it can communicate with the underworld.

Where does the sun go after it sinks under the horizon? The owl is the image of a god that governs the transformations between yin and yang, which means that it also governs the transformations between life and death. The owl's name, *xuan* bird, can either be interpreted as black, or as a bird with rolling eyes, because *xuan* has the meaning of "rolling" as in the word "xuanyun" (dizzy). The name "*xuan* bird" might have been inspired by these types of evidence.

More evidence can be found in people's lives. In the Sichuan dialect, the owl is called "gui che" (ghost cart). On one hand, this term draws attention to the connection between the owl and the underworld. On the other, it implies that the owl's eyes can roll like a cartwheel. The owl has another name, "gulu bird" (rolling bird). Its eyes are rolling, like the cycle of life and death, the alternation of yin and yang, and the rebirth of life. The Shang people worship the *xuan* bird, and we have finally understood, that their totem is not the swallow, but the owl. This exquisite bronze object was made by pouring molten bronze into a mold. It represents the highest level of art and craft techniques in the Shang dynasty and the pinnacle of the Chinese bronze tradition.

Fig. 3.18 The owl sculpture in the Tomb of Fu Hao

One of the two aforementioned owl sculptures is in the city of Zhengzhou, and it is the treasure of the Henan Museum. The other was welcomed into the collection of the National Museum of China in Beijing, where it is also a treasure of the museum.

The Poly Art Museum, located on the east second ring road in Beijing, purchases Chinese cultural relics from overseas regardless of the cost. What is the most famous artifact that it has purchased? The beast heads which were originally in the Old Summer Palace. The Poly Art Museum bought an exquisite bronze utensil of the Western Zhou dynasty, which is called the Pengji phoenix bird wine vessel (see Fig. 3.19). We can see it on display now. It is still in a bird shape and is still a wine vessel, but its image has completely changed from the owl to the phoenix. Another smaller phoenix stands on its back. When we see this exquisite bronze in the museum, bought at a very high price, we can see that the owl worship was no longer popular in the Western Zhou dynasty. A change of dynasties changes everything that follows. The previous dynasty's sacred object can no longer be sacred. To justify that, the Zhou rulers made up a story called the Phoenix Sings at Qishan: When the phoenix appears in the territory where the Zhou people settle, it means that the Mandate of Heaven has changed in favor of the Zhou. The revolution of King Wu of Zhou and the execution of the last king of the Shang dynasty were both driven by the belief in the myth of the phoenix singing at Qishan.

Fig. 3.19 The Pengji phoenix bird wine vessel. The photo was taken at Poly Art Museum, Beijing

This type of phenomenon in art history cannot be understood simply from the perspective of art appreciation. Back in the Shang dynasty we can find similar bronze vessels. The Shanghai Museum has one called the Xiao You (owl wine vessel) (see Fig. 3.20). One body, two heads, two sides connected as one. This design is from some 5,000 years old double owl-headed jade pendant of the Hongshan culture. It seems that before the Shang dynasty, the Chinese people worshiped the owl, which is very clear from the fourth tier of evidence.

Now we have discussed the animal totems and the plant totems. Lastly, there is the number worship. I have taken the main points from the book *Zhongguo Gudai Shenmi Shuzi* (*Mysterious Numbers of Ancient China* 中国古代神秘数字). How do numbers become sacred? How do they become symbols in the daily life of our ancestors? In the past, people like to use patterned numerals. If you read All Men are Brothers and Journey to the West, you will find repeated numbers such as 36, 72 and 108. These are set numbers, and their meanings have no connection with mathematics; rather they are connected with culture and belief. Non-Chinese might not be able to fully understand the numbers in All Men are Brothers. The Chinese philosopher Zhuangzi said that the Yellow Emperor had 72 mol. Lay people would not understand that these numbers are multiples of 12. 12 and 13 are both mystical numbers. Earlier mystical numbers are one, two, three, four, five, six, seven, nine and ten. In Japan, eight is the most mystical number. We Chinese like to have eight in

Fig. 3.20 The owl wine vessel of the Shang dynasty, unearthed from Tomb 229 from North Miaopu, Anyang in 1999

our phone numbers, but in ancient times, eight was not very sacred. The most sacred number is five. "Yin, Yang and the Five Elements," and "Five Emperors" both used this number. When we understand the number worship, we can decode certain parts of the Chinese culture.

Let's talk about the totem "one." Can you tell what is the original shape of the number one "壹"? It is "壶," the man-made vessel that imitates the shape of the gourd, the natural vessel (see Fig. 3.21). A lid and a vessel. The ancient intellectual history equals the "way" with "one," then how does "two" come into being? The gourd is the natural form of "壹" (one). In Chinese mythology, the sky and the earth were divided from a whole. How was that represented in the Chinese characters? We found two characters: "剖" in "解剖" (dissection), and "判" in "判案" (judging cases). Both contain a radical that means "the knife." Chinese people prefer things that are whole and unbroken. Dissecting in the middle, the above is the sky, and the below is the earth. Walking out in the middle are the gods *Fuxi* (male) and *Nüwa* (female). That is what Laozi described by "one begets two, two begets three, and three begets the ten thousand things." Laozi is not a philosopher in the Western sense. In China, the metaphysical finds its root in the physical. We can find the prototype of this in the gourd, which is most often used as a ladle. The ladle is an everyday household item in China. How do you make a gourd ladle? You cut a standing gourd in the middle. This illustrates the principle that "one begets two," that the root of two

3 The Flying Dragon and the Dancing Phoenix: Chinese Totem Myths

Fig. 3.21 The red clay gourd bottle of the Yangshao culture

lies in the one. Once one explains the one 壹, is it necessary to explain 贰 (two)? The prototype of "two" should be evident without explanation. The Chinese characters are the best examples of totems. When you can understand the original form of a Chinese character, this is the most convenient way to find the origin of the totem.

Let us summarize what we have covered so far. I discussed ten books in total, which can be summarized by 24 Chinese characters: 中国物象、社稷精神、示为祀、戈为戎、姬姜从女王、鸮熊(枭雄)变凤龙 (*Zhongguo wuxiang, sheji jingshen, shi wei si, ge wei rong, jijiang cong nuwang, xiao xiong bian feng long*). These are rhymed lines that contain all the discussed Chinese characters and totems, meaning the forms in China, earth and state, rice and spirit, radicals meaning sacrifice and weapon, the radical meaning female in Emperors Yan and Huangs' names, and the transformation of owl and bear into phoenix and dragon. The phrases "shi wei si" and "ge wei rong" tell us that that there are two extremely important symbols among the Chinese characters seen above: the radical "示" *shi* meaning 祀 (*si*, sacrifice), and "戈" *ge* meaning "戎" (*rong*, weapon). *Zuo Zhuan* 左传 states that the two most important things in a state are sacrifices and warfare. Today sacrifice is basically nowhere to be found, but in the pre-Qin period, sacrifice was always the most important thing, because victory in war is dependent on which side the god stands. Therefore, the sacrifice activities that connect the gods and man become the prototype of the core encoding process in the creation of Chinese characters. That is what the claimed equivalence of "示" (*shi* show, reveal, instruct) and "祀" (*si*, sacrifice) and "戈" (*ge*, dagger) and "戎" (*rong*, weapon) is all about. In order to clarify the source of the dragon and the phoenix, we discussed a series of recent archaeological discoveries, most of which were jade carvings. Now let me explain the traditional Chinese character *guo* 國 (state). In the middle is *ge* 戈 (weapon). The four walls guard the national treasure, which is jade. What are the most important things among the ancient Chinese totems? Based on current studies, nothing is more important than jade. In the two characters "物象" (*wuxiang*, objective image), if the characters are analyzed individually, "物" contains the "牛" (cow) radical, and "象" contains the "象" (elephant) radical. If you turn the character "象" 90 degrees counterclockwise, you can tell that it is an elephant. Why do the Chinese use the largest animal on land to represent all forms? That is the Chinese ancestors' easiest way to create characters. The Book of Changes has a term: "create symbols from objective beings." So almost all the Chinese characters can be traced back to prototypes, which provide clues to the totems' meanings. The phrase 姬姜从女王 *jijiang cong nuwang* (The names of the Yellow Emperor and the Flame Emperor contain the radical that is related to females) refers to the relationship between the Yellow Emperor and the Flame Emperor. One was surnamed 姬 and the other was surnamed 姜. Both characters contain the radical that signifies "female." "王" here is pronounced in the fourth tone and it is a verb, meaning to claim the crown. Both the Yellow Emperor and the Flame Emperor are related to females, so they became ancient kings and ancestors of the Chinese people. We will save the principles here for later discussion.

Next, please have a look at the following images. Why does the character "國" *guo* (state) contain the most important Chinese totems? We didn't understand it in the past, but many Chinese characters contain "戈" *ge*. "戈" is a weapon that only the ancient Chinese had. The earliest 戈 discovered is over 4,000 years old. People also discovered city wall relics dating to 4,000 years ago in Shimao Ancient City in Shenmu, Shaanxi (see Fig. 3.22), which was ranked one of the ten greatest archaeologist discoveries in the world in 2013.

An outer wall surrounds an inner wall in the Hetao region along the Yellow River in northern Shaanxi. That corresponds precisely to the character "國" *guo*. The earliest "戈" was made of jade, and it was not used in warfare but rather as a symbol of power. "国" is not a modern simplified character for "國," but rather a folk character from before the Qing dynasty. Both "國" and "国" make sense in terms of images. One uses weapons to guard the city wall, the other tells us that the treasure in the city wall is jade. Now we have pretty much come to understand the Chinese totems. People discovered such jade implements in the inter stone crevasse of the ancient city wall of Shimao Ancient City (see Fig. 3.23). They represent the totem jade implements of ancient China from a time earlier than the oracle bone script and earlier than the Xia, Shang and Zhou dynasties. They bring us associations with the macro tradition that are extremely rich. We knew nothing about it before, but today we have discovered jade implements in the city walls. Please take a moment to think about this.

The jade carvings of the Xinglongwa culture are earlier than the dragon and phoenix totems. They are dated to some 8,000 years ago and were found in Chifeng, Inner Mongolia. This is a jade pendant that was discovered in very early days (see

3 The Flying Dragon and the Dancing Phoenix: Chinese Totem Myths

Fig. 3.22 Shimao Ancient City in Shenmu, Shaanxi

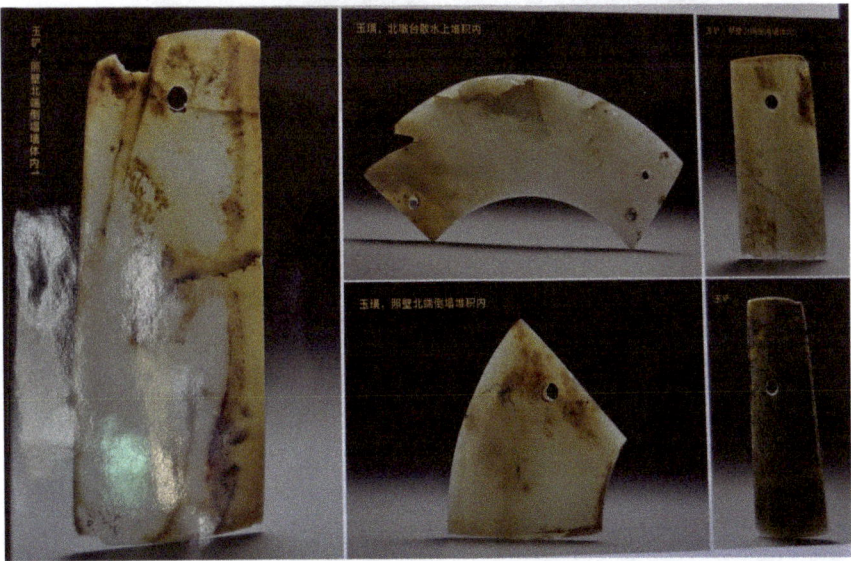

Fig. 3.23 Jade objects found in the city wall

Fig. 3.24). No corrosion was found on it after such a long time, so our ancestors attributed sacred connotations to it.

Back to the dragon and the phoenix. The earliest dragon and phoenix were made of jade. This is because the physical material itself was a totem, and could be understood

Fig. 3.24 The earliest jade implements were found in Xinglongwa, dated to some 8,000 years ago

Fig. 3.25 The dragon-shaped jade pendant of the Eastern Zhou dynasty unearthed in Jingzhou, Hubei

as a totem upon a totem, worship on the top of worship. The Eastern Zhou jade pendant unearthed in Jingzhou, Hubei is made of white jade, and is extremely beautiful (see Fig. 3.25). We have already discussed the relationship between the dragon and mankind. In the pre-Qin era, the dragon was a supernatural tool of communication. To communicate with the gods, people had to wear a jade pendant in the shape of a dragon. It wasn't until after the First Emperor of Qin that people made a connection between the dragon and the emperor.

The earliest prototype of the phoenix is also found in jade carvings. Many scholars have called a jade implement of the Hongshan culture the "jade phoenix." There are even speculations that it is the first jade phoenix to appear in ancient China, dated to over 5,000 years ago. The images on jade often represent the totem of that time.

Fig. 3.26 The C-shaped dragon, a landmark sculpture in front of the Aurora Pavilion of the 2010 Shanghai Expo, was modeled after a jade dragon of the Hongshan culture of over 5,000 years ago. The jade dragon was unearthed in Chifeng, Inner Mongolia

Fig. 3.27 The jade bear dragon unearthed in the Tomb of Fu Hao of the Shang dynasty

During the 2010 World Expo, a C-shaped dragon (see Fig. 3.26) was placed in front of the Zhendan Pavilion, which was different from the dragon we are familiar with. How did the bear become the dragon? We can tell from the object introduced below. In 1976, a precious jade carving was unearthed in the Tomb of Fu Hao of the Shang dynasty, which was called the Jade Dragon (see Fig. 3.27). No matter how one looks at it resembles a beast of prey.

Actually, this piece is a combination of three animals: the head of a bear, the antlers of a deer, and the body of a snake. The bear head appears because the bear goes into hibernation in winter. The deer antlers symbolize longevity and an everlasting life, as they fall off in the winter and grow back in the spring and summer. The body is that of a snake, because the snake also hibernates in winter, and it sheds its skin. The ancient Chinese believed that these phenomena all represent rejuvenation and revival, so they combined these three life-energy animals to form the dragon. Later, the dragon was added claws, so we weren't able to recognize its prototypes. But actually, the dragon is the result of the said combination.

The combination of mythological animals and sacred materials is what constitutes our Chinese tradition. If you wear a jade object believed to guard you and bring you peace, that represents a tradition of 8,000 years ago that persisted until today.

Chapter 4
Emperors Yan and Huang, Our Ancestors: Chinese Ancestor Myths

Shuxian Ye

Emperor Yan and Emperor Huang (the Yellow Emperor) are usually considered as Chinese people's ancestors. Their names are "Shennong" and "Xuanyuan", respectively, and they both are the earliest emperors in ancient legends. But from the perspective of history studies, the two emperors cannot be accepted by academia as real figures in historical texts. What is the reality about Chinese ancestry culture? How do the Chinese people piece together evidence from cultural codes to prove that their ancestors had truly existed? This chapter mainly discusses the genealogy of Chinese people's ancestors through historical criticism and archaeological examination. We attempt to provide a clearer framework for the questions that remain nebulous. By historical criticism, we mainly refer to a major school of thoughts: the Doubting Antiquity School or Yigupai. This school became prominent around the late Qing and the early Republic of China era, as Western concepts about the discipline of history entered China. The Doubting Antiquity School decided that the established historical genealogy recorded by Sima Qian and Ban Gu, especially the Three Sovereigns and Five Emperors, was fake history made up by the later generations. They thought that the earliest histories were untrustworthy. Only the history after Eastern Zhou dynasty was reliable. So, even the validity of the Xia, Shang and Zhou dynasties was doubted, not to mention the era of the Emperors Yan and Huang. Today, after nearly a century, what is the new response to this question? That is our topic for this lecture.

We mainly use the quadruple evidence method. The legends in question happened in a time that was much earlier than the written language, so they went beyond the scope of the written texts. We all know that the oracle bone script came into existence only over 3,000 years ago, and the Yellow Emperor lived over 5,000 years ago. It is true that what happened over 5,000 years ago cannot be found in written records, given the written language only came into being around 2,000–3,000 years ago. So we mainly rely on the new evidence from archaeological discoveries to reconstruct the historical genealogy in the Emperors Yan and Huang's era. That is the reason we highlight the quadruple evidence method. Another point: we had only been talking about the Emperors of Yan and Huang, but they are the Han people's ancestors. As China is home to multiple peoples, only talking about the Han Chinese's ancestors means we are excluding the ancestors of other peoples. Therefore, a new terminology is created: "三祖" (three ancestors), meaning the Yan Emperor, the Yellow Emperor and Chiyou. Chiyou is considered the ancestor of the ethnic minority groups in Southern China. The change from two ancestors to three ancestors reflects the progress with the times and the unity of all ethnic groups.

I want to introduce two museums. The first one is China Three Ancestors Museum in Zhuolu, Hebei, where the Yan and Huang Emperors fought Chiyou. This museum honors the three emperors as the common ancestors of the Chinese nation (see Fig. 4.1). This museum mainly displays the folk legends, which are accompanied by some unearthed objects. The second museum is also newly built. Located on a hill in Jianping town, Chaoyang city, Liaoning province, the Niuheliang Archaeological Site Museum is said to be "the largest prehistoric site museum in the world" (see Fig. 4.2). If you visit North China, you can spend some time at this museum. It preserves the authentic ruins over 5,000 years ago. Especially, there is a temple that deserves our attention. The goddess worshiped in the temple is considered "the female ancestor of the Han Chinese". There are also numerous tomb sites, from

Fig. 4.1 China Three Ancestors Museum

Fig. 4.2 Niuheliang Archaeological Site Museum

which many exquisite jade implements were unearthed. The C-shaped jade dragon from this Museum belongs to the Hongshan Culture, which dates back to 5,000 years ago at the Niuheliang site and Chifeng area in the east of Inner Mongolia. Before the 21st century, we didn't even know the existence of those displayed in the two museums. Today I hope I can lead you to a new world. Whether the exhibits were actually left behind by the Emperors of Yan and Huang, that is not important. What is important is that these exhibits represent the origin of civilization dating back 5,000 years ago. That's what we want to emphasize on.

This lecture will cover four issues. I'll make an introduction to the theories and methodologies. Why did we take a different approach to the Emperors of Yan and Huang from previous scholarship? Because we have advanced with the times in knowledge and ideas. In theory, we categorize the cultural traditions into the macro tradition and the micro tradition. In the past, only the micro tradition was available for cultural studies. We had nothing else to refer to except for the complex or even contradictory records in the ancient books.

Today, we discovered the macro tradition, which started earlier than the oracle bone script and was nowhere to be found in written records. In the past, we didn't have any reference materials. Now, the large amount of unearthed objects, pictures and symbols can restore the mythological system of that era to some extent. The binary system of the macro and micro tradition is a communication vehicle based on symbols. Part of the system is comprised of the Chinese characters, and the other part has no characters. Written texts are important, but they appeared too late for us to study the cultural traditions dating back over 5,000 years ago. For us, the era that is not recorded in writing belongs to the macro tradition. Literary anthropology integrates the literary texts with anthropology studies and creates a new knowledge system. Since the macro tradition existed before the written language, it definitely didn't rely on the written language. In fact, many of the Chinese characters were derived directly from the mythological imagination and symbols. Now, we understand the sequence and depth of cultural traditions. We call the written contents the surface culture, and the pre-writing contents the macro tradition at a deeper level.

We talked about the quadruple evidence method before. The first tier is written literature. We used to rely solely on literature to do research without a clear idea of the authenticity and credibility of the written records. Now, putting them in perspective, the written records are like the statements submitted to court. Facing different statements from the plaintiff and the defendant, the judge has to evaluate the physical evidence, which are more objective. The second tier refers to the unearthed scripts, which had been missing from the books. From the oracle bone script and the bronze script to the bamboo script, now we have a rich collection of evidence from this source. To form a new perspective on knowledge, we must rely on the newly unearthed scripts. What if the newly unearthed oracle bone script contradicts the written records passed down through the ages in regard to the Shang dynasty? Of course, we have to give more weight to the oracle bone scripts. The oracle bone scripts were carved on tortoise shells and bones and buried underground three thousand years ago. Judging from the books burned by the Emperor Qin, the books that were passed down were mostly compiled during the Han dynasty. There was a huge gap in between. The earliest antique books in the library were hand-copied in the Han dynasty, which was just 2,000 years ago. The oracle bone scripts, on the contrary, were at least 3,300 years old. So, the second tier of evidence is much more reliable than the first. But before the newly unearthed scripts, we could only rely on the ancient books. The third tier of evidence is the anthropologists' forte. Their research objects were mostly peoples without the written language. How to reconstruct history and culture sans written language? History books were out of the question, so anthropologists can only conduct field research. The genesis and exodus told by the tribe elders contain historical information, from which we can discover traces of historical reality. Today, we consider the oral history and the ritual performance, which belong to intangible cultural heritage, as the third tier of evidence. In some aspects, it effectively addresses the questions that cannot be solved by the first and second tiers of evidence. The third and the fourth tiers of evidence corroborate each other in many ways. The most important evidence contains information of the time period. We call it the fourth tier of evidence, which mainly contains archaeological sites, artifacts and images. With those evidence, our exploration of the era of the Emperors of Yan and Huang can far surpass our predecessors'. When the era of the Doubting Antiquity School, there was no mature archaeological material to use on a large scale, so the School had the slogan: "Down the idols from the Three Sovereigns and Five Emperors era." Despite that, it is necessary to reconstruct historical facts so that we know what they are actually like.

The next four points are about the era of the Emperors of Yan and Huang. First, according to the micro tradition of textual records, "descendants of the Emperors of Yan and Huang" was first known as "Huang and Yan" and later it became "Yan and Huang." The two ancestors waged a war in the prehistorical era, called "the Battle of Banquan." The general belief is that it happened in the south of Zhuolu County, Hebei. Some other people think it is in Yuncheng County, Shanxi province. In a word, it is definitely a battle launched in North China. The winning side is Emperor Huang, and the losing side is Emperor Yan. Therefore, the earliest term put the Yellow Emperor in front of the Emperor Yan. Instead of "descendants of the Emperors of Yan and Huang, the term was "descendants of the Emperors Huang and Yan." *Discourse of the States: Zhou Part II* 国语·周语下 holds that the descendants of the Huaxia (Han Chinese) ethnic group are called "descendants of the Emperors of Huang and Yan" when it was discussing the Xia's genealogy. That is the earliest available written text on "Huang and Yan." "Huang and Yan" later turned into "descendants of the Emperors of Huang and Yan," "descendants of the Yellow Emperor," and "descendants of the Emperors of Yan and Huang." Comparatively speaking, "descendants of the Emperors of Yan and Huang" came into being relatively late. It didn't become popular until late Qing to the period of the Republic of China. We live in a modern context, so the most familiar term for us is "descendants of the Emperors of Yan and Huang." Why was the Emperor of Huang placed in front of the Emperor of Yan? As an old Chinese saying goes, "the winner is the king." When two parties are fighting, the winning side is respected as No.1 and put in the front.

Where were the two prehistoric emperors born? Why were their surnames Ji and Jiang, respectively? According to *Discourse of the States: Jin* 国语·晋语, "Shaodian married a woman from the Youjiao clan, who later gave birth to the Emperor Huang and the Emperor Yan. The Emperor Huang grew up by the Ji river, and the Emperor Yan by the Jiang river. They grew up to have different virtues, so Emperor Huang's family name is Ji, and Emperor Yan's family name is Jiang. The two emperors waged war on each other, because of different virtues." *Discourse of the States* dates back to the Eastern Zhou dynasty. People then thought of their ancestors as brothers of the same mother. Scholars today generally think that Ji river is Qishui River at Wugong, Shaanxi, and Jiang river is Qingjiang River at Baoji in the same province. The two rivers are geographically close, both in the West of Guanzhong Plain. The two surnames, Ji and Jiang, seem to come from the two rivers. That is the earliest record of the birthplaces and sources of surnames of the Emperors of Yan and Huang. How to understand "virtue" in "they grew up to have different virtues"? Is it related to virtues and morals? Why did they fight each other? Because they had different "virtues". It seems that "virtues" were close to mythological beliefs and had nothing to do with morality in today's sense. Just like Confucius said in *Analects*: "Heaven bestows virtues to me 天生德于予", virtues are inborn. Because each clan has different totem worship and idol, different ethnic groups have different cultural affiliation: that is the cause of conflicts. With "virtue," the ancient Chinese referred to the inborn godly characters and power. Each ethnic group relates its ancestors to a holy figure. The two ancestors were related to different holy figures. About their mother Youjiao clan, the only record was found in *Classic of Mountains and Seas* 山海经. The sixth book in Volume 5 of *Classic of Mountains and Seas* 山海经·中次六经 records that "The peak of Gaodi Mountain is called Pingfeng, facing Yiluo in the South and Gucheng Mountain in the East…At Pingfeng there is a two-headed god who is built like a human. The god's name is Jiaochong, and is the leader of the Ao worm living in the house of bees 缟羝山之首,曰平逢之山,南望伊洛,东望谷城之山…有神焉,其状如人而二首,名曰骄虫,是为螫虫,实惟蜜蜂之庐…" Scholars today suspect that Youjiao is a clan that worshiped the bees. They intermarried with Youxiong tribe and gave birth to the Emperors of Yan and Huang. *Classic of Mountains and Seas* was considered a book of mythologies and legends in the ancient times. Nobody used it for textual research. But today, scholars are trying to explore the regional cultural resources. Mengjin town in Luoyang city, Henan province is considered the location of the Pingfeng Mountain. In 2011, it hosted the "Seminar on the Culture of the Emperor Yan and Huang's Mother's Hometown". In spite of everything people might say, this place is indeed in central China, and Youjiao's hometown was found here. Whether to believe in it, it is up to everyone's judgment.

We have introduced the state Youxiong. "Xiong" (the bear) did not come out of thin air, but can be traced back to the prehistoric culture. *Lushi* 路史 especially mentioned that the Youxiong state is in Xinzheng, Henan, where the Zhengzhou Airport is located. Nowadays a Yellow Emperor Square has been built in Xinzheng, on which stood a gigantic *ding* (bronze sacrificial vessel). The three legs are the images of standing bears (see Fig. 4.3). The local people still remember the king of the Youxiong state and its holy bear. That is also a must-go place for overseas Chinese to recognize and acknowledge their roots and ancestors.

Fig. 4.3 Bear-foot Ding at Xinzheng, hometown of the Yellow Emperor

About the "descendants of the Emperors of Yan and Huang," we have discussed the earliest record about the two emperors, including their birthplaces and how they got their surnames. Talking about the sacrifice for them, *Records of the Grand Historian: the Book of Feng and Shan Sacrifice* 史记·封禅书 recorded that "Duke Ling of Qin worshiped the Yellow Emperor at Wuyang Upper Zhi, and worshiped the Emperor Yan at Lower Zhi 秦灵公作吴阳上畤,祭黄帝;作下畤,祭炎帝." The two venues were of equal importance, but the Yellow Emperor preceded the Emperor Yan, so the Yellow Emperor was worshipped at the Upper Zhi while the Emperor Yan the Lower Zhi. The two emperors were considered by the Qin people as their common ancestors. Both the First Emperor of Qin, who had united China, and the Han dynasty inherited this ancestry. The three pieces of documents we quoted all put the Yellow Emperor in front of the Emperor Yan. Obviously, "Emperor Yan and Huang" came into being later. Moreover, this phrase was not popular until the late Qing and Republic period. During the Opium War in the Qing dynasty, the foreign invaders shattered the country and families, so the phrase "descendants of the Emperors of Yan and Huang" became popular. Later, the Revolution of 1911 stressed the Yellow Emperor in an effort to overthrow the Qing dynasty, so that phrase was upheld, and it remained our slogan in safeguarding our home and country until the end of the Anti-Japanese War. Fengjia Qiu, the Taiwan-born patriotic poet wrote: "As descendants of the Emperors Yan and Huang, we are devoted to our ancestors, like the birds missing their home forest, and the fallen leaves attached to their roots 人生亦有祖,谁非黄炎孙? 归鸟思故林,落叶恋本根." In the context of fighting foreign invasion and overthrowing the Qing's reign, the phrase "descendants of the Emperors of Yan and Huang" became the consensus in the discourse since the modern China. That is the basic answer to the question on the Emperors of Yan and Huang as ancestors in the micro tradition.

The Yellow Emperor is also known as Youxiong, and he founded a state which is also called Youxiong with the bear as its totem. We will discuss this question again later. Here we want to discuss the surname Jiang of the Emperor Yan. The character "Jiang" (姜) is composed of a goat (羊) and a woman (女). In the oracle bone script, "jiang" (姜) is interchangeable with "qiang" (羌), which we know is an ethnic minority group. *Shuowen Jiezi* (*Explaining Graphs and Analyzing Characters* 说文解字) interprets "qiang" as "shepards of the West". *Shuowen Jiezi* is a dictionary in the Han dynasty. The information contained came from the River Qingjiang area in Baoji, Shaanxi, and Tianshui region of Gansu, which is at the midstream of the Wei River. The upstream of the Wei River is in Weiyuan town, Gansu. Further west is the boundary of Gansu and Qinghai, which boasts developed nomadic culture in the northwest China. The distribution of people named after Jiang in literature is similar to that of the nomadic culture today. If the Han ethnic group is the result of the interaction and integration of two branches, then the one after the Yellow Emperor represents the farming culture, which centers around the Central Plain and is part of the Yangshao culture in the prehistoric era. The main food crop was millet. Wheat wasn't planted until 4,000 years ago. It was a crop from the West, which is represented by Emperor Yan. He is related to the culture of China's west. The earliest nomadic culture in the world appeared in today's central Asia. Nomads do not have fixed habitation, which strongly contributed to the spread of their culture.

The Han Chinese have three concepts: the true, the good and the beautiful (真善美). Two of the three characters are related to goat (羊). Shen Xu, author of China's first dictionary Shuowen Jiezi mentioned above, interprets "美" as "the big goat is beautiful" (see Fig. 4.4). For farmers, the meat is a rare delicacy, but for nomads, it is common food. As the farmers' diet was mostly millet, their nutrition was poor. But

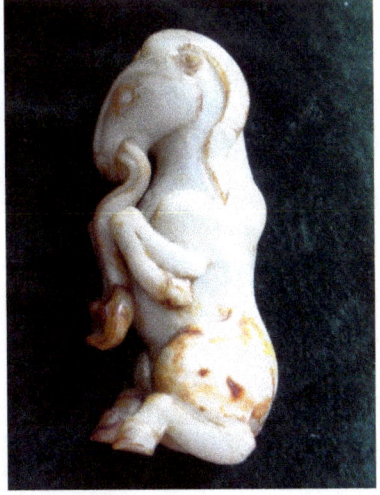

Fig. 4.4 The big goat is beautiful. This is a jade goat, with a pendant Ruyi in its mouth. It means "yangyang deyi" 洋洋得意, a Chinese idiom meaning "being content with oneself"

with lamb, their nutrition would get much better. Meat in ancient China was rare. My family was sent off to North Shaanxi during the Culture Revolution, so I have life experience about that place. There, one can only eat meat during New Year's. Except that, one only has the millet to eat. The wheat flour was basically nowhere to be found. At such a place as the Loess Plateau, the Western nomadic culture is especially needed as a supplement. So the notion that "the big goat is beautiful" is relevant to the fatness of the goat.

Nowadays people try to avoid high cholesterol, so they detest the white meat. But people in the ancient times loved it. Children from rich families were called "Gao Liang kids." As "Gao" refers to animal fat, this name means that they could eat meat every day. Du Fu depicted such a scene in his poem: "Through the vermilion gates one can smell the delicious wine and meat, while people are frozen to death by the road." "Big goat is beautiful" manifests the influence of the Western nomadic culture on the farming culture. The concept of beauty started with taste.

One can find much evidence on goat worship. The goat is one of the twelve Zodiac signs. The reason is that the characters for goat ("羊") and for auspice ("祥") are the same. To the Chinese, auspice is important. The goat represents auspice. Many items prove the existence of the goat totem. For example, the dragon may have a goat's head. In the 1980s, the goat-headed dragon made of bronze was unearthed at the Three Stars Mound at the north of Chengdu (see Fig. 4.5). It clearly shows the goat horns. Moreover, it has the goatee. Some say it is a dragon, and some disagree. But the goat totem is closely related to the Jiang Qiang culture. The nomadic culture in the west significantly enriched the farming culture in central China. Many of the descendants of the Emperors of Yan and Huang as we know today are actually descendants of the Qiang people who entered the central China very early. The other Qiang people, who are in South Gansu and North Sichuan, were those blocked outside the central

Fig. 4.5 A goat-headed dragon bronze vessel unearthed in the Three Stars Mound

plain. Jiang was an important family name in ancient China. As a significant source of the Han Chinese, half of them had that family name.

The second question we are going to address is a key one: what exactly is the totem of the Yellow Emperor? The different virtues of the Emperors Yan and Huang actually mean that their divine strength was different, which means that their totems were different. The Yellow Emperor's totem was directly related to his name. He was known as Xuanyuan or Youxiong. How should we understand the two names? No satisfactory explanation was given in the past. We have two records about the earliest names of the Yellow Emperor. The first record was found in *Bamboo Annals* 竹书纪年 of the Warring States period: "The Yellow Emperor lived in Youxiong after he took the throne in the first year 黄帝轩辕氏, 元年帝即位, 居有熊." Here, Youxiong seems a place name. In *Records of the Grand Historian: Five Emperors* 史记·五帝本纪, the first one recorded was the Yellow Emperor. The author Sima Qian wrote: "The Yellow Emperor is the son of Shaodian. His surname is Gongsun and his given name is Xuanyuan 黄帝者, 少典之子, 姓公孙, 名轩辕." He also wrote: "The Yellow Emperor, Shun and Yu share the same surname, yet they have different dynastic appellations respectively to promote their virtues. So the Yellow Emperor was called Youxiong; Emperor Zhuanxu was Gaoyang; Emperor Ku was Gaoxin; Emperor Yao, Taotang; Emperor Shun was Youyu; and Emperor Yu was Xiahou; and he had also the surname Si 自黄帝至舜、禹, 皆同姓, 而异其国号, 以章明德。故黄帝为有熊, 帝颛顼为高阳, 帝喾为高辛, 帝尧为陶唐, 帝舜为有虞, 帝禹为夏后, 而别氏, 姓姒氏." According to *Collected Annotation of the Records of the Grand Historian* 史记集解, the Yellow Emperor was the king of the Youxiong State, and Youxiong was considered the state title under the reign of the Yellow Emperor. Based on that, all the ancestors of the Han Chinese were descendants of the Yellow Emperor and thus were related. Even the Xiongnu in the north were considered descendants of the Yellow Emperor.

The question is: what do Xuanyuan and Youxiong refer to? How to interpret the two names? Let's use the myth of the symmetry of the heaven and the man. Both the characters of "Xuan Yuan" (轩辕) are related to "vehicle" (车), as both contain this radical. Among the mythologies related to the Yellow Emperor, a story tells how he invented the south-pointing chariot. During a battle between the Yellow Emperor and Chiyou, the later conjured up a storm to get the Yellow Emperor's army disoriented. So the Yellow Emperor invented the chariot, not to carry goods but to point directions. Another legend goes that the Yellow Emperor has four faces. He is considered the god residing at the center of the four directions, east, west, north and south, so he faces all of them. When can we find the south-pointing chariot? Let's find out through Bronze bear chariot unearthed from the tomb of Qin Dukes in Li county, Gansu (see Fig. 4.6) province. Bronze had been used for either tools and weapons or sacrificial vessels. Such discoveries with mythological significance were very rare. Just now we know that during the reign of the Duke of Ling of Qin, the Emperors of Yan and Huang were treated as objects for ancestral veneration and temples were built for this purpose. In the culture of the Qin people, this piece of antique is relevant to Youxiong. It is a square bronze chariot with a bird standing on each of its corners. Sitting in the middle was a drayman, and behind him in the middle of the chariot is a godly bear.

Fig. 4.6 Bronze bear chariot unearthed from the tomb of Qin Dukes in Li, Gansu

Four *chihu* (螭虎) were lying at the sides. Obviously, this one-on-four relationship represents the center and the four directors. The four chihus and the four birds are all guarding the bear in the middle. This relationship is shown clearly through their positions. Although it wasn't accompanied by texts, and we don't know what it was for, we are certain that there was a model when it was built, and the designer had a mythological archetype in mind.

Though we only have this one isolated piece of antique, we can conclude that this chariot was not for carrying goods or people, but to represent an astronomical phenomenon. What is it? My answer is the Big Dipper. Rotating around the pole throughout the year, the Big Dipper can help people determine the east, west, south and north. That is an example of how our ancestors in the agricultural society determine the growing season by observing the sky. That is best proven by the saying "when the Big Dipper points to the east, the whole world is in spring." The following is a picture of the Big Dipper provided by Beijing Planetarium. In Chinese, besides being a container, the bowl of the dipper also means "the carriage," and the handle means the shaft (see Fig. 4.7). The Polaris is the center of sky, circled by other stars. Confucius used the Polaris as a metaphor in *Lunyu (Analects of Confucius)*: "(he)

Fig. 4.7 Xuanyuan as the vehicle: Mythological imagery of the Polaris Carriage of the Emperor, a picture of the Big Dipper provided by Beijing Planetarium

may be compared to the north polar star, which keeps its place and all the stars turn towards it." This north polar star refers to the highest governor on earth.

It is clear now that we can find the roots for Youxiong and Xuanyuan in the imagination of the oneness of the sky and the people. Our ancestor's imagination is not groundless, even seemingly so. This picture is a mythological illustration of the Polaris Carriage of the Emperor drawn by the Beijing Planetarium. Now we've answered the questions about the radical of "vehicle" in the name Xuanyuan, and Polaris Carriage of the Emperor. Aided by the bronze bear chariot unearthed from the tomb of Qin Dukes in Li, Gansu, we can understand the correspondence between the king of Youxiong and the yellow Emperor and Xuanyuan. It shows how important the quadruple evidence method is in solving the unsolvable problems. Even the ancient scholars weren't able to examine the valuable pre-Qin antique with mythological symbolism.

How to explain Youxiong in the sky? If you are familiar with Greek mythology, you will know that the Little Dipper is part of the mythological system. It looks like a bear cub after you connecting several stars. Together with the Big Dipper, they are both in our childhood imagination. So did people in ancient times. They thought of the stars as gods in the appearance of bears. So on earth, bears were imagined to be gods descending to the world. That is the second tier of evidence, which is more effective than the first tier. One article in the *Chu Silk Manuscript* 楚帛书 unearthed in Changsha is on China's Genesis. After the sky was separated from the earth, the earliest characters came out were "heavenly bear". Some people say it is "big bear". The bear is the archetype of the ancestor we found. How to understand the heavenly bear? We have to look into the third tier of evidence, culture preserved by word of mouth. It contains the cultural memory that remains unchanged over thousands of years, from which we can seek evidence. The third tier of evidence contains the oral and intangible cultural heritage. The Hezhe people and Oroqen people in north China have mythologies in which the bear was their ancestral totem. The bear is usually related to the gods or is the avatar of a god. These legends sound like mythologies, but are remnants of the heavenly bear culture in the prehistoric age. As is known to all, the hunting age predates the agricultural age. The hunting people's mythology is the most original and the oldest mythology.

From the manifestation of heavenly gods in the culture of the ethnic minority group, we can understand how the idea of heavenly bear originated. Twenty thousand years ago, Asia and Americas were not separated by the Bering Strait yet but were connected. The American Indians' ancestors arrived in the Americas from here. Their second most important totem was the bear. The American Indian sorcerer's sacrifice costume (see Fig. 4.8) was covered by the bear pattern, which means the heavenly bear descended to the earth. All the positive energy is shown through clothing.

In previous paragraphs, we discussed the three-hole jade carving with two bear heads from the Hongshan culture (see Fig. 4.9). We don't know what they are called after unearthing it. With two bear heads at the sides and three round holes in the middle, it is addressed as an altered jade *huang*. The standard jade *huang* has one dragonhead on each side. The character for "rainbow" in the oracle bone script is a bend shape with a dragonhead on each side. In people's imagination, the rainbow

Fig. 4.8 The American Indian sorcerer's sacrifice costume with bear faces

Fig. 4.9 Three-hole jade with two bear heads, Hongshan culture

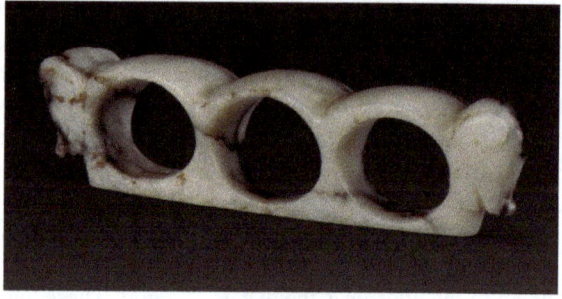

is a bridge connecting the sky and the earth. People going up to heaven and gods descending to the earth have to have this connecting bridge.

The jade represents the sky deity. The mythological intention of the jade *huang* is to use jade to build a rainbow bridge. Scholars on oracle bone script think that the rainbow appears only after the storm. We also have the song: Without the wind and the rain, how can we find the rainbow? The ancient people believe that when the water in the sky falls to the ground during a heaven rain, the sky deity feels thirsty, and then he would turn to a double-head dragon descending to the earth to drink. The character for rainbow in oracle bone script depicts the dragon drink with a wide-open mouth. With this background knowledge, one can easily understand this jade carving is a symbolic ritual instrument to connect the human and the deity.

Based on the above, we know that the idea of the heavenly bear is definitely not the brainchild of the writer of the *Chu Silk Manuscript* from the Warring States period. It represents the inheritance of the macro tradition imagination that was not

Fig. 4.10 Heavenly bear and god, Shaman and Nuo

recorded in texts. In the past, there was no way to study it. Now we can let the antiques speak for themselves. The key is to master the technique of interpretation. Some people would ask: why wearing a bear costume makes one a deity? If you don't believe it, please look at this picture. It is a sorcerer's standard costume in north China (see Fig. 4.10). Just wearing the bearskin means the arrival of the sky deity, nothing else needed. Shaman dance means that the sorcerer turns into deity after wearing the bearskin. Now we see how powerful the third tier of evidence can interpret antiques and literature. Everyone who has seen live ritual dancing knows what it means, so I will not spare time on it. Who is not familiar with these? Only the modern people living in the city, not familiar with the folk culture, his root in mythological imagination is severed. Luckily, this ancient cultural tradition can still be found in Shaman dance in North China. This is a Shaman dance costume taken in a museum at Vladivostok (see Fig. 4.11). Vladivostok used to be China's territory in the Tang and Qing dynasties. In North China lived the Shaman-worshiping ethnic minority group. This Shaman dance costume has only one bear at the hem. The dance must be accompanied by ritual tools and music, representing the descending of the god. One bear or dozens, it works in the same vein as both stands for the connection of the bear and the sky deity.

Can archeology prove the existence of the Xia dynasty? The Xia dynasty poses a complicated academic problem for it is even earlier than the oracle bone script. No writing system was invented by then, and people had no idea where its capital was and how the country was passed from one emperor to the next. But among the objects and pictures that were earlier than the Shang dynasty, we found an antique that was equivalent to the national emblem of the Xia dynasty. Yanshi Erlitou Relic Site at Henan is generally considered the location of the capital city of the late Xia dynasty. This witnessed the discovery of the most prestigious piece of antique: the bear-shaped bronze plate with turquoise (see Fig. 4.12). The bronze plate is studded

Fig. 4.11 A Shaman sculpture in the dancing costume in a museum at Vladivostok

Fig. 4.12 The bear-shaped bronze plate studded with turquoise, unearthed in Erlitou, Henan

with hundreds of pieces of fine turquoise, in a shape that is the same as the Shamanic sacred plate, a ritual tool. Some say the plate shape is a tiger, and some say it is a fox. But actually, it is a bear. At that time, people were just beginning to use this metal, and this plate was among the earliest-made bronze objects in Central China. The turquoise represents the blue sky; therefore, it is a sacred object to represent the sky deity. People of the Xia dynasty are descendants of Zhuanxu, grandson of the Yellow Emperor. So they were related to the Youxiong clan.

Bears seldom appeared in the literature but are often spotted in the fourth tier of evidence. From 8,000 years ago to the present-day antique jade factories, this image remains constant. It means that it is related to the memories about the bear totem.

Fig. 4.13 Gilded Double Bears of the West Han dynasty unearthed in Anhui

In the West Han dynasty, the golden bear was produced. We all know that gold is very precious. If the bear stands for clumsiness and is derogatory in language, people wouldn't use the gold to make bears (see Fig. 4.13). This is the culture loss: the macro tradition is getting away from us while we are only living in the micro tradition.

Nowadays, people use "bear" to refer to "stupidity". Bear is used as a derogatory term. That shows that the sacred bear is completely forgotten in the agricultural age of the micro tradition. There is a break in cultural tradition as time goes by. Therefore, we cannot interpret the ancient mythology with today's cultural ideas. Facing these unearthed objects, we must first be respectful. This is not bear, but the descended deity. After knowing this, let me give you an example from the second tier of evidence: *Rongchengshi* 容成氏, a bamboo slip manuscript of the Chu state during the Warring States period, collected by Shanghai Museum (see Fig. 4.14).

Fig. 4.14 *Rongchengshi*, the bamboo-slip manuscript of the Chu state, Shanghai Museum

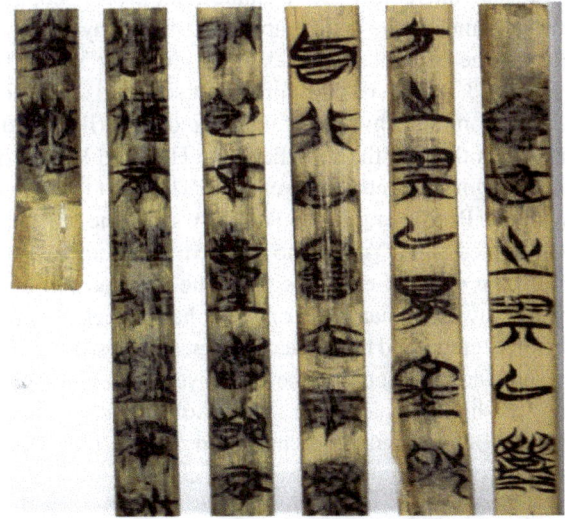

The manuscript tells that Emperor Yu is widely loved because he tames the flood. To recognize people from different places, he uses five flags with totems. "The flag with the sun goes to the East; the moon, the West; the snake, the South; the bear, the Center; and the bird, the North." Yu's own flag has the bear, the central animal. It completely agrees with the fourth tier of evidence. No evidence can be more convincing. By now, the question about the Xia dynasty is solved, and so is the question about the bear totem. The national flag is actually from the totem. A totem pole in front of a tribe is similar to a national flag. The clansmen of the Yellow Emperor still feel affiliated with the Xia flag. Also, the bear-shaped bronze plate with turquoise actually serves the function of the national emblem. With the national flag and the national emblem, what is left to doubt about? Actually, mythology about Emperor Yu is related to the bear. The best explanation is found in the *Classic of Mountains and Seas*.

Some hold that the four corners flags are not important and only the center flag is. That is nowhere near the truth. Without the four corners, there is no center. Without the center, there are no corners. They are interdependent. Figuring out the relationship between the four directions and the center is our Chinese's archetypal experience. That is how China, or the center country (Zhongguo), is named. "Zhong" was originally written as a pole with a flag waving on top. It symbolized people surrounding the center of the sacrifice ceremony, and referred to the central space.

The discovery of the central bear flag is indeed striking to the modern people. We can roughly imagine how the Emperor Yu's bear flag looks like through the Han stone relief antiques two thousand years ago. Flags in the ancient times share something similar throughout the history. Here we show a stone relief from the Han dynasty that is preserved in the Temple of Confucius in Linyi, Shandong: the image of the standing sacred bear (see Fig. 4.15).

The third question is important too. That is, if we look at the characters of "姬" (Ji, surname of the Yellow Emperor) and "姜" (Jiang, surname of Emperor Yan), they share the radical "女" (female). In the past people had been perplexed: why did the surnames of the great emperors contain anything that was related to femininity? How come both the surnames of the Emperor Yan and the Yellow Emperor contain "female"? The micro tradition didn't solve this problem. The character for surname "姓" is combined by "女" (female) and "生" (life). Today, we have many surnames, as shown through the so-called "the Hundred Family Surnames." However, during the pre-Qin era, there were very few. The most important surnames came from totem symbols. People of the Zhou dynasty share the "Ji" surname. Their female ancestor was named Jiang Yuan, who married into Zhou as a woman from an outside clan. From the view of eugenics, only the descendants of the interracial marriage can be healthy. So a man from one clan has to seek a woman born in another clan. But different clans tend to fight each other, so it poses a challenge to the interracial lovers. Here we need to mention a new discovery in the international academic circle: Before the worship of male deities, the whole world actually only worshiped the female deities. Before civilization appeared, people only worshipped the goddesses. That was discovered in the late twentieth century.

4 Emperors Yan and Huang, Our Ancestors: Chinese Ancestor Myths

In China, a clay sculpture of a goddess was unearthed in the Niuheliang Goddess Temple site in Jianping, Liaoning. Only her eyeballs were covered by jade (see Fig. 4.16). She is considered the ancestor of the Chinese women.

No male deities were found in this temple. Only goddesses. Another discovery is the stone relief goddess found in Hebei that is approximately 7,000 years old (see Fig. 4.17). How can we be certain that it was a female? Just look at her body. Her

Fig. 4.15 The image of the standing sacred bear

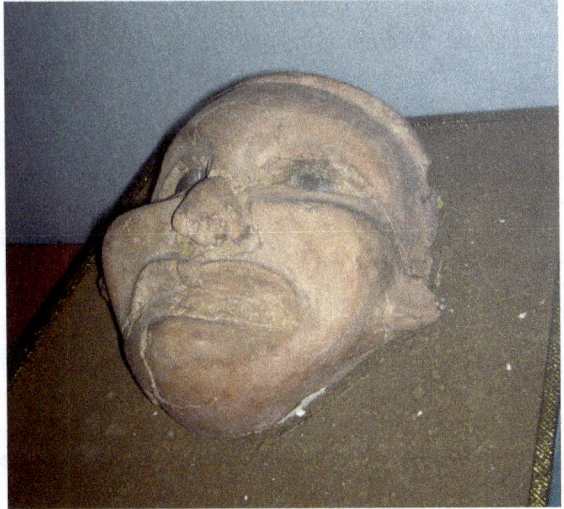

Fig. 4.16 A clay goddess sculpture in the Niuheliang Goddess Temple site

Fig. 4.17 A stone relief goddess sculpture in Hebei, approximately 7,000 years ago

big belly and plump breasts are highlighted, to stress the function of fertility. By observation, the ancient people knew that all babies came from women's bellies. Entering the agricultural society, farmers had the same imagination, thinking that the earth was their mother. In "yin and yang," "yin" (female) comes before "yang" (male). That matches the subject of our research. Why do the two ancient surnames "Ji" and "Jiang" share the radical of "femininity"? A possible reason is that in a polygamy society, a newborn's father was nowhere to be found, so the child would be given the mother's surname. Such things are still happening among the Naxi people in Yunnan province. In the prehistoric age, female worship was not uncommon.

An important academic discovery in the 20th century, as we just mentioned, was that 5,000 years ago, before the written language, if there was a deity, that must have been a goddess. The goddesses mostly stood for mother and fertility. *Did God Have a Wife?* is an English book (see Fig. 4.18). It poses a question to Christianity, which worships the holy trinity: the Father, the Son and the Holy Spirit. This book asks the question: did God have a wife? It is not a novel subtitled "Archaeology and Folk Religion in Ancient Israel," it poses a question, which is answered by a picture on the title: "God did not only have a wife, but God himself had been a woman." The cover image is an unearthed sculpture that existed before Judaism came into being in Israel. From the hair you will know that it is a goddess sculpture. It is an academic book and an epitome of the rediscovery of goddess in the twentieth century, which influenced culture as a whole. *Da Vinci Code*, a bestseller novel, is also a result of this movement. If you read the novel after *Did God Have a Wife*, you will understand that the novel is on the goddess worship which had been lost in patriarchy.

Fig. 4.18 *Did God have a wife?*

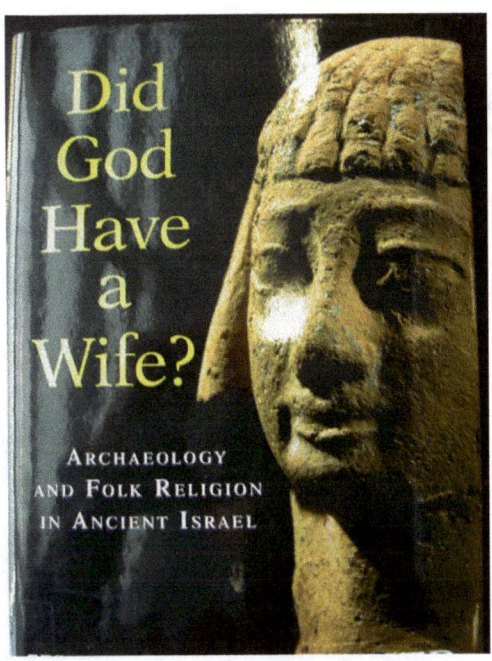

Coming back to the question of the Emperors of Yan and Huang, there are quite a few achievements in Chinese goddess research. Two books, *The Goddess with a Thousand Faces* (2004) and *The Living Goddess* (2008), are responses of the Chinese academic community to the major international academic discovery. Here in the Chinese Academy of Social Sciences, we are finishing a project called "A Mythological Research of the Sources of the Chinese Civilization". The majority of the research findings have been published. Among them is a translated book, *The Language of the Goddess*, by the late American archaeologist Dr. Marija Gimbutas. Dr. Gimbutas was the most notable scholar on goddess civilization research. This book tells us, goddess worship had existed for over tens of thousands of years. Only in the civilized society with the written language was the goddess worship replaced and forgotten. As today's writers, screenwriters and directors are striving to find new topics, goddess worship is indeed the deepest root in the cultural macro tradition. If a goddess' sculpture has a swollen abdomen with breasts highlighted, it usually means fertility and child-rearing. It represents mother worship.

In Linxi county, Inner Mongolia, people unearthed a female stone sculpture that is 8,000 years old (see Fig. 4.19). It ushered in Chinese sculpture history. Still it depicts a goddess, which was 3,000 years earlier than the Emperors of Yan and Huang's era. At that time, people had no idea what male deities look like. Now, we finally find our real root of ancestry. That is a reflection of matrilineality long, long ago. The goddesses are represented by symbols. Except for the human-shaped symbols that are readily recognizable, there are eight animal images too. What are the eight animals?

Fig. 4.19 The female stone sculpture in Linxi, Inner Mongolia, approximately 8,000 years ago

Fig. 4.20 The stone bear of Xinglongwa Culture, unearthed in Linxi, Inner Mongolia, approximately 8,000 years ago

In Linxi, except for the stone relief goddesses, people found stone bears (see Fig. 4.20). The No. 1 fierce beast is the bear. Among insects, the bee represents fertility. *Erya*'s definition of the bear is "a hibernating animal". It disappears in the fall and winter and revives in the summer.

Although the bear is big, its sleeping pattern throughout the year makes people think that it can revive after death. Therefore, it has enormous energy. So the character of the bear ("熊") is based on "能" (energy), meaning the energy of life that can repair itself and revive after death. The Xinglongwa culture of Linxi shows that people were

Fig. 4.21 A bear jaw unearthed in the Goddess Temple in Niuheliang

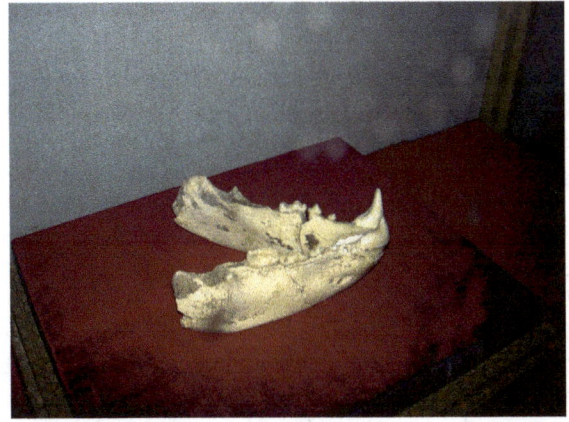

growing millet 8,000 years ago, and they worshiped goddess and bear. So it is not strange that a bear skull was unearthed from the 5,000-year-old Niuheliang Goddess Temple (see Fig. 4.21). The Niuheliang Goddess temple contains both the goddess and the bear. The eight animals that represent the goddess include the eagle, the night bird of prey, and the owl which especially stands for the transformation of the yin and yang. For the same reason, the pig and the frog also represent the goddess. The Chinese Nobel Laureate Mr. Mo Yan wrote a novel on family planning. The title is

Fig. 4.22 A bear-shaped lamp of the Vinča culture

Frog, because the frog can once lay hundreds of eggs. So these symbols carry certain connotations, and none of them is random.

In the Goddess Temple at Niuheliang there was a clay bear head. Very clearly, we can see the lower half of the bear's canine. In the Goddess Temple we can find the evidence for both the goddess and the sacred bear, which verifies Dr. Gimbutas' goddess worshiping civilization hypothesis.

Outside the Han Chinese culture, people have found many prehistoric antiques in the shapes of bears, frogs and owls on the Eurasia continent. Dr. Gimbutas included a bear-shaped lamp from the former Yogoslavia over 6,000 years ago in her book, *The Language of the Goddess* (see Fig. 4.22). The bear body represents energy. People at that time lit the oil lamp, hoping the light could last longer and the energy could be perpetual supply. The bear has a lot of fat in its body. Especially before it goes into hibernation, it seeks food all over the mountain to store energy. So the bear represents energy and is most suitable as the symbol of the lamp.

The bear sculpture of the Vinča culture is a two-footed bear like a standing person (see Fig. 4.23), not a four-footed animal. It belongs to the former Yugoslavia culture. You all know by a glance. There are many such sculptures in the region of the ancient Chinese culture, those that are from four to five thousand years ago. After the Shang dynasty, many of such antiques were unearthed. For example, the jade bear from the Tomb of Fu Hao in Anyang, Henan (see Fig. 4.24) is in a sitting position that looks exactly like a human.

Where has the goddess-worshiping culture gone? Why is it lost in today's cultural memory? Because it was fought over, conquered and replaced by a patriarchy culture around 4,000 years ago. Dr. Gimbutas believes that on the Eurasia continent lived the

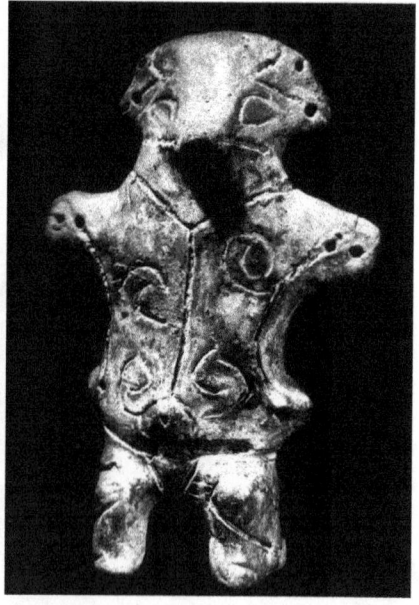

Fig. 4.23 A bear sculpture of the Vinča culture

Fig. 4.24 Jade bears from the Tomb of Fu Hao in Anyang, Henan

nomadic Kurgan people. Different from the farming culture, the nomadic people lived wherever the water and grass was. They fought battles as they went to different places, so this martial group upheld male heroes. The patriarchy society of the nomadic people was the enemy of the goddess civilization on the Eurasia continent. Originated in the Caucasus Mountains region, the Indo-European people spread to the Central Europe, South Asia, West Europe, India and Persia. What is the distinctive characteristic of the nomadic people? It is their mobile lifestyle. Their society is structured around spontaneity. Pulling up the tent and off on the way they go. The farming people, on the other hand, have a lot of bonds they cannot sever, but not the nomadic people. Therefore, the nomadic people were very aggressive and they usually won the battles with the farming people. How is the ancestor of the nomadic people expressed in the Chinese culture? One of the Chinese people's three ancestors is Chiyou. According to relevant documents, Chiyou was a very powerful man because of his most advanced weapons and he was the first to use the metal weapon.

In the ancient time, soldiers fought hand-to-hand with metal weapons. Chiyou's image came from the faraway nomadic culture. As shown on a piece of Han stone relief picture, Chiyou was a "兵" (*bing*) god with metal weapons (see Fig. 4.25). The meaning of "兵" (*bing*) is twofold: one is soldiers, the other is weapons used for wars. It was significant achievement for Chiyou to become the bing god. For the people who farmed, the nomads are foreign and advanced people who used metal weapons. Although Chiyou was conquered by the Yellow Emperor in our mythological narrative, he was a great man in our old, collective memory. Chiyou's image on the Han stone relief told us that the metal weapons were relevant to the cultural movements in the West and the cultural influence from the West. *Taiping Yulan* (the Imperial Reader or Readings of the Taiping Era) 太平御览 quoted *Longyu Hetu* 龙鱼河图: "Chiyou is one of the eighty-one brothers. They speak human language but have beast bodies, bronze heads and iron foreheads 蚩尤兄弟八十一人, 并兽身人语, 铜头铁额." That means they were impervious to swords and blades. Volume 100 of *Yunji Qiqian* 云笈七签 stated: "Eighty brothers with bronze heads and iron foreheads 兄弟八十人, 铜头铁额." The metal armor was imagined as the skin of people from the West. In the ancient times, the character "戎" means a person holding a metal dagger-ax (戈).

Fig. 4.25 Chiyou Holding Weapons in stone relief from the Han dynasty

蚩尤（汉代石刻）

Today's archaeological records show that bronze was firstly produced in the area from West Asia to East Europe, which was about 2,000 years earlier than in China. The Erlitou bronze plate, the earliest in China, has just 4,000 years of history. West Asia has at least 5,000 years of history producing bronze. Metal weapons, warhorses and horse carts were all introduced from Central Asia. On their course they must have passed through the prairie area, so China's Xinjiang area entered the Bronze Age and the Iron Age earlier than the Central Plains. Iron was rarely used before the Spring and Autumn period. During wars, the weapons were made of bronze. Not much bronze was used during the Erlitou culture period, either. Central Asia is home to the domestic horse. Before the Shang dynasty, the central plain area of China didn't have a single domestic horse. All horses were introduced from the West afterwards. Therefore, Chiyou with its bronze head, iron forehead and metal weapons is a strong enemy from the West in central Chinese's imagination.

The above is our interpretation of the Chinese's three ancestors' cultural identity from the perspective of archeology. Lastly, the fourth question is about the weapons in the era of the Yellow Emperor. That is an important piece of information from *Yue Jue Shu* 越绝书. *Yue Jue Shu* is a book from the East Han dynasty. It proposed four eras through the evolution of ancient weapons. In the time of Xuanyuan and Shennong, the weapons were made of stone; in the era of the Yellow Emperor, weapons were made of jade; in Dayu's time, bronze was used; and in the Warring States, iron was used. The four eras roughly follow the chronological order, accompanied by four materials, respectively. Many myths and legends as we see now are obviously made up by modern people, especially the legend about the Yellow Emperor rising to heaven after casting a cauldron. If the Yellow Emperor existed 5,000 years ago, it was impossible to cast a giant cauldron with metal. We can veto the validity of this legend if we examine it with the quadruple evidence method. It was mixed with something that has not existed in the era of the Yellow Emperor. In the era of the Yellow Emperor, weapons were made of jade. Is that convincing? From today's perspective, it is very convincing. From stone, jade, bronze to iron, that is a continuum, like the dominoes. In the mid- and late-Neolithic age, the earliest residents in East Asia selected a holy stone, that was jade. Was it used in weapons? In the past people had no idea, but now, numerous materials tell us that jade weapons really existed. It was around 5,000 years ago; a large number of jade weapons were made. In *Yue Jue Shu*, a person named Fenghuzi said the same thing. As we see today, the texts indeed hid cultural information of the macro tradition. The materials used in ancient weapons strictly follow the order of stone, jade, bronze and iron, one appeared earlier than the following.

A 5,000-year-old grave in Northern China was opened. People discovered the Goddess Temple in Jianping, Liaoning, and unearthed a grave with only jade implements as burial objects. The owner of this grave was also recovered. The Aurora Pavilion of the 2010 Shanghai Expo showed the image of the grave owner: he wears a jade crown, a jade bracelet, and jade on his waist. He holds a jade weapon in his hand. It is a jade battle-ax, representing the military power and judiciary power, and the right to kill and wage wars (see Fig. 4.26). Since this is the image of a tribe leader 5,000 years ago, is it a representation of the jade weapon era?

Fig. 4.26 Jade Tomb in Hongshan Culture: the tomb owner and the restoration image

Fig. 4.27 Restored images of the king and queen displayed in Liangzhu Museum

By the outer ring road in Hangzhou, there is a newly built Liangzhu Museum. The museum was built on the site of an ancient kingdom 5,000 years ago. With the help of models, the museum recreated the images of the king and queen back then (see Fig. 4.27). The museum created an image of the king in a yellow gown, but how could the king have a yellow gown? The jade objects in their hands were made in 1:1 scale of the unearthed antiques. The sizes and specifications were exactly the same. They layered jade necklaces on their necks and wore jade bracelets. The king held a jade battle-ax in his left hand. That is the jade culture from the lower reaches of the Yangtze River to Hangzhou Bay. Southern China and Northern China had been unified by the jade culture as early as 5,000 years ago. The existence of the jade weapon is the most convincing fourth tier of evidence. If people ask me what jade weapons we are able to see today, I'd say the jade battle-axe, which is copied from the stone axe. To figure out if a jade implement is a weapon or a ritual object, we need to find out if it is a tool people used in the past, or a ritual object with no evidence of use. How to distinguish that? We can take a look at the blade. If it was used as a tool, the blade would show the damages. But if the blade was smooth without any trace of use, it was a ritual object. The practical tool is an ax, and the symbolic object is a jade battle-ax. That is the beginning of the Chinese ritual culture. The earliest jade weapon was not intended for a kill, but a symbol of power. The new archaeological discovery of the 21st century revealed two systems of jade weapons centered around the jade axes. The dagger-ax first came into being in jade. The jade dagger-ax unearthed in the Erlitou site (see Fig. 4.28) dates back over 3,000 years. An earlier one was unearthed in Shimao, north of Shaanxi, and is 4,000 years old. During the time of the jade dagger-ax, which lasted from over 5,000 years ago to over 3,000 years ago, it was very difficult to find the jade weapons which were earlier than the Yellow Emperor.

In other words, before the bronze weapons, jade weapons had existed for a long time among the Chinese. If the Yellow Emperor and Emperor Yan lived around

4 Emperors Yan and Huang, Our Ancestors: Chinese Ancestor Myths 101

Fig. 4.28 The jade dagger-ax unearthed in the Erlitou site, dating back to over 3,000 years ago

Fig. 4.29 Jade battle-ax unearthed in the Yangshao Culture Tomb at Xipo, Lingbao

5,000 years ago, then the tombs shown in the following two pictures (see Figs. 4.29 and 4.30) predate Yellow Emperor's time.

The two pictures were shot in the newly discovered tomb sites in the 21st century. The first tomb site belongs to the Yangshao culture at Xipo, Lingbao, Henan. Opened in 2004, these tombs were built 5,300 years ago. There unearthed a dozen jade battle-axes. All were made of dark serpentine jade (see Fig. 4.29). The good jade as we modern people know of is tremolite, which was not used in Central China over 5,000 years ago. These jade battle-axes were ritual objects in the shape of a weapon. Therefore, the legend of jade weapons era is proven by the prehistoric high-level graves in Central China. Among the over 100 graves, only one or two unearthed jade objects. These graves' owners generally had high social status, such as those in the ruling class of a society.

The picture below shows the Lingjiatan Tomb at Hanshan, Anhui discovered by the Yangtze River in 2007. Although only three years apart from the Xipo Tomb unearthed in 2004, Lingjiatan Tomb contained an amazingly large number of jade

Fig. 4.30 Panorama of Tomb 07M23 at Lingjiatan, Hanshan, Anhui

objects. Over 300 jade objects were unearthed in one tomb, mainly jade battle-axes (see Fig. 4.30). The tomb owner lay on numerous white jade battle-axes. None showed evidence of use on tools. Those were symbols of power and status that were meant for the dead to use in heaven in the coming life. Therefore, the era of jade weapons covered not only in parts of China. From West Liao River in the North, to the Yellow River region in Northeast China, to the Yangtze River and Huai River regions in the South, jade culture was found in all those places. They were unified by the jade battle-ax. When a ruler died, local people had to make over one hundred jade battle-axes as burial objects. What a large workload! Cutting, selecting, drilling and polishing, how much time would it take! It is the equivalent of China's Three Gorges Project 5,300 years ago. When the whole society serves one person, obviously the gap between the haves and the have-nots had been formed. When we saw the 23th tomb of Lingjiatan opened in 2007 in Hanshan, Anhui, we finally understand why the quadruple evidence method can prove what Fenghuzi, the sword forger, said: "In the era of the Yellow Emperor, weapons were made of jade." Only people in the 21st century were able to see the jade weapons. Not the scholars in the past. They weren't even able to imagine it.

So far, we have gone through the four key points in the era of our ancestors Emperors of Yan and Huang. Now we make a brief summary. We piece together the background for our research from the legends of the Emperors of Yan and Huang 5,000 years ago. Against this background, we can try to make a judgment with the quadruple evidence method and see which myths and legends are reliable, and which are imagined. "In the era of the Yellow Emperor, weapons were made of jade", we used the objects unearthed in North and South China as examples, to show that our current method of studying the prehistoric culture has advanced with the times, and can solve the puzzles that perplexed our ancestors. Our limited time and energy should be used in the materials that can be proven and shown. If we break free of the restraints of the micro tradition of texts, we can gain new knowledge on the macro tradition of history. The things that we were unable to see are now placed in the museums. That is why I recommended two museums in the very beginning. Words can't capture the image of the Han Chinese 5,000 years ago. Only when one puts oneself to the site of 5,000 years ago, can one understand that the long history of the Han Chinese is no joke.

Chinese civilization had never been broken off. The Chinese today still love jade as they buy and wear it. That is a practice passed down from 8,000 years ago, which provides a basis to decode the micro tradition. The jade culture can spread all over China, just like a religion. That is a deeply embedded macro tradition. As we study the mythology about our ancestors, we go beyond the Doubting Antiquity School's suspicion about the prehistory and reveal the true historic image of that period. If we only rely on the written words, there are too many hidden things. History includes the things that are hidden and forgotten by words and narratives. The fourth tier of evidence can rebuild the lost history of civilization.

Chapter 5
Sages Yao and Shun: Chinese Sage Myths

Shuxian Ye

For prehistoric mythology about totems and ancestors, we try to show to the public what has been proven by the latest discoveries. In the past, if we were to discuss Yao and Shun, we were limited to the two emperors only. Today, to discuss Yao and Shun, we have to rely on three most reliable archaeological sites: Taosi, Shimao and Lajia. They are all archaeological discoveries of major significance over the past two decades. Twenty years ago, hardly anyone had heard of these sites. Today, no evidence is more powerful than they are in the discussion of Yao and Shun's era. Please take a look at the two pictures from the Shimao site at Shenmu, Shaanxi. The first picture shows a jade head pendant that was collected at the site, and the second shows an almost identical pendant from the personal collection of a local collector (see Fig. 5.1). A few questions were raised: Why does the Chinese imagination of the country have to be related to a special material? What does China look like at its earliest stage? Focusing on China 4,000 years ago, let's take a look at what the cultural heritage of the Yao and Shun era can prove today.

The era of Yao and Shun is jointly created by the Confucians and the Mohists. In their minds, that era is an ideal era governed by sage kings. We are familiar with Confucius's praise of Yao in the *Analects*: Great indeed was Yao as a sovereign 大哉, 尧之为君也. In the Spring and Autumn era, when people thought of the origin of the Chinese culture, they said "uphold Yao and Shun's teachings as instructions from ancestors and follow the social system under the reign of Wen and Wu emperors of Zhou as the constitution 祖述尧舜, 宪章文武." In the Confucian sage kings' genealogy, Yao and Shun are two of the six kings in four generations. The other four are Yu, who curbed the flood, King Tang of Shang, King Wen of Zhou, and King Wu of Zhou. The six sage kings are the wisest, and they represent the lifeline of the Han Chinese in Confucius' heart. People generally have no objection to Confucius' words, so there was seldom any doubt to Yao and Shun's historical status after Confucius set the tone. Du Fu (712–770, poet in the Tang dynasty) wrote in a poem: "致君尧舜上, 再使风俗淳 I would make my lord greater than Yao or Shun, and cause our customs again to be pure (Translated by Prof. Stephen Owen)." That era has been an ideal world of peace and prosperity in Confucians' memory. How ideal was it?

Fig. 5.1 Jade head pendants at the Shimao site of Shenmu, Shaanxi

People did not lock doors at night, and there were no wars. That was the Chinese people's utopia. When poets and scholars of latter times mention Yao and Shun, they had nothing but praises. Chairman Mao also wrote it in his poem: "Six Hundred Thousand Chinese are all like Shun and Yao 六亿神州尽舜尧." In this lecture, I list five pieces of reference materials that are the latest research findings on this topic. They are *An Illustrated History of the Origin of Chinese Civilization*, *A Mythological Research on the Sources of the Chinese Civilization*, *Abdication of Yao and Shun: A Historical Structuring of the Confucian Political Myths*, *A Research in the Yao and Shun's Legends*, and *The Heir and the Sage*. In particular, *A Research in the Yao and Shun's Legends* 尧舜传说研究 is Dr. Yongchao Chen's Ph.D. thesis from Nanjing Normal University. It systematically examined the myths and legends since Yao and Shun by regions. The fifth reference book is written by Dr. Sarah Allan, an American scholar of ancient China. Using structuralism, her analysis of the legends of Yao and Shun's abdication is very authoritative. Through the five pieces of reference, we put the historical questions about the Yao and Shun's myths to the forefront of literature and historical studies.

About Yao and Shun, the earliest and most authoritative record comes from *The Canon of Yao* 尧典 from *The Book of Documents* 尚书, China's first history book. There used to be a *Canon of Shun* 舜典, but it was lost in history. Some other people think that the second half of *The Canon of Yao* is *The Canon of Shun*, because that way, both of the sage kings' deeds would be included in the first article of the book. "格于上下" "在璇玑玉衡" "辑五瑞" "班瑞于群后"[1] from these words, you can get a rough idea of the rulers' top concerns 4,000 years ago. *The Book of Documents* enjoyed such a high status that almost all the ancient scholars were able to recite it. It started with "曰若稽古". To annotate the four characters, a classic commentator of the Han dynasty wrote 100,000 words. That is how esoteric *The Book of Documents*

---

[1]Translator's note: These phrases are all relevant to jade, as explained later in this lecture.

is. After the Emperor Qin burnt books, *The Book of Documents* was put together by scholars of the Han dynasty from their memories, so it contained many problems. For us, it is a written document left by the Han scholars to record the admiring narratives of the Confucianists, Mohists and scholars of other schools about the prehistoric era. The four words describing Yao "格于上下" still pose a puzzle for modern people. Similar texts were accepted as truth in ancient times but were viewed with a doubting glance by the modern scholars. They held that the records before the Xia, Shang and Zhou dynasties were unreliable, and were fabricated by the later generations. This opinion had been held by the Doubting Antiquity School headed by Jiegang Gu for almost a century, from 1920s to present. Today, the mainstream historians are still arguing over whether the prehistoric materials are mythology or history. To reconcile this disagreement, we coin a word "mythistory". Myths may not be fake, and history may not be true. History is nothing but narratives and expressions. Only those who lived in history knew what was real. If mythistory becomes a subject that can be partially researched and proven true, then which parts can be examined? Using two tiers of evidence method, we can find ample evidence for "格于上下". Confucianism upholds 格物致知 (seek knowledge by examining the way things operate) as the goal for studying, as written in *The Doctrine of the Mean* 中庸. The modern meaning of "格" (square) does not make sense here. However, in the Chinese bronze inscriptions, such narratives as "格于上下" (examine the up and down), "格于皇天" (examine the royal heaven), "格于百神" (examine the hundreds of gods) are not rare at all. Therefore, the narrative source of *The Canon of Yao* goes way back. Those words are obviously not something that could be conjured up from the imagination of later generations. The second tier of evidence refers to the unearthed texts such as the oracle bone scripts, bronze inscriptions, the bamboo slip manuscript and the stone inscriptions, which the ancient scholars might not have seen. The two-fold evidence supported by the bronze inscriptions sufficiently proves that the first thing remembered about the two sage kings in *The Canon of Yao* was the divinity of their rights. Politics is not only about administration but is centered on a predestined purpose. 格于上下 means connecting with gods. In order to establish sovereignty on earth, one has to address the connection between the heaven and the earth. From the perspective of myths, we can slowly understand those expressions. More importantly, we discovered what our ancestors used in order to examine gods and the heaven (格于上下, 格于皇天, 格于百神). 格 is comprised of 木 and 各. 木 refers to the trees reaching out to the sky, meaning connecting the heaven and the earth. 各 is often used to refer to clouds, which symbolizes the communication, interaction and movement between the heaven and the earth. Once we find what 格 represented in the narratives of the Yao and Shun's era, we realize that something is indeed worthy of our attention.

"在璇玑玉衡,以齐七政。肆类于上帝,禋于六宗,望于山川,遍于群神。辑五瑞。既月乃日,觐四岳群牧,班瑞于群后 (By observing the astronomical instruments Xuanji and Yuheng, the priest sorts through the seven governing affairs. Then he prays to god, heaven, earth, four seasons, mountains and other spirits, and collects the five kinds of jade as tokens. He picks an auspicious month and day to meet the emperor and officials, and distribute those jade tokens to the princes)" means that after

Yao retired, Shun took the throne. Ancient scholars have provided clear annotations to "辑五瑞" (collect five jade ritual pieces) and "班瑞于群后" (distribute the jade tokens to princes). These phrases contain a frequently used word "瑞" which is also adopted in many Chinese names, as you may find when flipping over a roster. Why? Because it means "reaching heaven and earth", and connecting gods and humans. In the past, we did not know if such things had ever happened. But now, based on the unearthed objects, we are pretty sure that 璇玑玉衡 refers to the Polaris. How come that 瑞, 璇 and 玑 all contain the radical 玉 (jade)? 璇玑 was also written as 瑞玑, so the ancient annotators thought they were all jade implements, the 玉璇玑 (jade *xuanji*) in ancient times. Before the archeological discoveries, people did not know what the 玉璇玑 (jade *xuanji*) was. Nowadays, people unearthed those objects from 4,000 years ago in many places, from the Shandong Peninsula to the middle reaches of the Yellow River. So, the question about 璇玑玉衡 from the era of Yao and Shun is answered by objects.

About Yao and Shun, there were two opposite views back in the pre-Qin era, but we were only familiar with the praise and admiration from Confucianists and Mohists. When rulers throughout China's dynasties passed their powers to their descendants, Yao passed his reign to Shun, who was not blood-related at all to Yao. Shun was a farmer, but was selected by Yao as successor because of his virtue. On the contrary, Yao's son Danzhu was exiled because of bad conduct. The abdication of the crown to a non-blood-related person had become a practice that the Confucianism scholars spoke highly of. Even today, some people think that it is primary democracy in the prehistoric era: as long as one has good characters, they can be emperors. Confucianism scholars have heaped praises on this practice. Here I provide you three quotations. The first one is from *Xunzi* 荀子: "Yao has virtues. Without a weapon, he made the Miao people honor his authority. He appointed Shun from the farming fields as his successor and then retired from his office 尧有德, 干戈不用三苗服。举舜畎亩, 任之天下身休息." At that time, if other groups had disagreements with the Han ethnic group, they would fight it out. But thanks to Yao's virtues, other groups would automatically come to show their respect without a fight at all. It was Yao who recommended the farmer Shun to take over his crown. Peace under heaven, that is in line with the Mohism principle of "no war" 非攻. The ancient Chinese' virtues can be reflected from that. So, some people thought that the abdication of the crown was created by Mohists. Next, I will present you with two views that you might find unfamiliar. In ancient books, some records are contradictory. Some think it was a good thing, and some think otherwise. As *Bamboo Annals* 竹书纪年 goes, "Shun imprisoned Yao, and then confined Danzhu to keep him from seeing his father 舜囚尧, 复偃塞丹朱, 使不与父相见也." It means that Yao did not give up his seat voluntarily, but was imprisoned by Shun who seized the throne and forbade him from seeing his son Danzhu. This view represents a weak voice in historical records, because Confucianism and Mohism's impact was too strong. If Confucius said nobody was greater than Yao, who dared to deny that? Let's look at a quote from *Han Feizi* 韩非子: "Shun coerced Yao to yield the throne, Yu coerced Shun, Tang exiled Jie, and King Wu attacked King Zhou of Shang. These four kings were subjects who killed their lords 舜逼尧, 禹逼舜, 汤放桀, 武王伐纣, 此四王者, 人臣

弑其君者也." The most serious crime in ancient times was 弑 *shi* (subjects killing their lords, or sons killing their fathers). It was high treason for a subject to kill his lord. To Han Feizi, the four kings all committed the crime of *shi* as they coerced the rightful kings to surrender the thrones to them. Jie and King Zhou had such bad names in the mainstream history, but to everyone's surprise, Han Feizi thought of Yao, Yu and Tang as no better.

Actually, the disputes in the ancient books over morality would lead nowhere. If Yao and Shun's era was earlier than the Xia dynasty, that would be over 4,000 years ago. In the past, we might not have been able to determine if politics at that time was based on democracy or wars, but today we are able to find some clues. Our methodology is from literary anthropology. While historical records can be viewed as literary texts, we need to use materials from multiple subjects to judge which parts are reliable and which are fabricated. How do we prove the *Canon of Yao* is true using the quadruple evidence method? We just mentioned that with the second tier of evidence provided in the bronze inscription, we understood that 格于上下 means communicating with gods. The most important activity, when communicating with gods, was the ritual. An essential object of the ritual was 瑞 *rui*, which was the holy jade sacrifice object. According to historical records, after Shun took the throne, the world was peaceful. Queen Mother of the West 西王母 came to the court to do him homage with jade ritual objects. According to *Guanzi* 管子, "Yao and Shun used the Yu clan's jade to rule the world 尧舜北用禹氏之玉而王天下." These contents can be proven true, because jade objects appeared four thousand years ago. Quality jade came from West China, and most people who transported jade were the nomadic ethnic minority groups at the Hexi area in the west. The Yu clan was very likely to be the Dayuezhi clan. Meanwhile, the abdication of the crown between Yao and Shun was proven false, as it might be a narrative jointly created by Confucianists and Mohists. Three newly discovered prehistorical sites reflected China's common problem four thousand years ago, which was the appearance and upgrade of violence. Violence was represented by wars and defense. During wars, there must be attacks and defenses. Around 4,000 years ago, a large number of city walls appeared in central China. Those walls were not for peaceful purposes, but for defense. When trying to figure out the true and the false, the quadruple evidence method would be effective. It helps us judge what can be proven and what is falsified in the ancient books. The abdication of the crown of Yao and Shun was created by Confucianism to condemn and hide the violence in the prehistoric era in the name of benevolence and morality, which was the value upheld by the scholars and history books of Confucianism and Mohism. They treated a falsified political myth as actual history in order to hide the cruel reality that is soaked in blood. Thus, the meritocracy and abdication of the crown in the prehistoric age became a mythistory that was constructed in a way that was hard to distinguish the true from the false. When was it constructed? Just as the hundreds of schools were rising during the Spring and Autumn period.

Another reference to today's discussion is a seminar held on December 12, 2015 by Institute of Archaeology, Chinese Academy of Social Sciences and Shanxi Culture Relics Bureau. In Xiangfen, south of Shanxi, a relics site called Taosi was founded, so the seminar was named "Taosi Site and Culture." Experts from the seminar determined that Taosi was the capital of Yao. They thought that Taosi culture highly matched the Yao's capital as recorded in literature. The discovery of this site proved that the middle Yellow River area had entered early civilization in the Yao era and formed the earliest China. I want to introduce three 4,000-year-old sites of China. One is at the upper reaches of the Yellow River in northwest China, one is at the Hetao region in the west, and another is at the south of Shanxi. The three, when connected, form the upper to middle reach of the Yellow River. Taosi was the first unearthed site among the three. The official archaeological report was released in December 2015, which named this place "Yaodu" (Yao's capital). Though released by a pretty authoritative institute, there was room for academic discussion. Where did Yao and Shun establish their capital? According to historical records, the capital was at Yangcheng. But several places bore the name of Yangcheng in ancient geography, and people didn't know which exactly was the capital. Now, archaeologists found a city of 2.8 million square meters which was in existence approximately the same time as the Yao and Shun's era. Geographically it was close to central China, and researchers thought it highly matched the description of Yangcheng. But there was no ironclad evidence. We now take it as a proven prehistoric hub in central China during archaeological discovery. Shanxi government highly values the Taosi site and determines to promote it as the capital of China in the early times. In comparison, the Yanshi Erlitou Relic Site at Henan was thought to be the remaining site of Xia's capital, but research proved that it was built in 1750 B.C., which was late Xia, instead of the early Xia. So now Taosi site was especially valued, because it was a major city that has over 4,000 years of history.

In 2007, we visited Taosi (see Fig. 5.2), where unearthed palaces, high-level grave, ritual and musical instruments, crocodile skin drum, mass-produced jade ritual

Fig. 5.2 Taosi

objects, and the earliest bronze ware. This was indeed an important site. Where is it located? We know that the Yellow River is shaped like the character "几", with a huge turn going south from the middle Inner Mongolia, passing the Hukou Waterfall, blocked by the Huashan Mountain in Shaanxi, and taking another 90° turn to the east. Shanxi is just on the east side of the "几". The Chinese saying "thirty years at the east of the river, and thirty years at the west" refers to Qin and Jin, which were two states at the opposite banks of the river. The Taosi site was at the bank of Fen River, an east branch of the Yellow River. This map has five squares, which mean the archaeological cultural distribution at the upper Yellow River region 3,000 years ago. How was the prehistoric culture related to the Han Chinese culture? How was the Han Chinese culture of the Yao and Shun's era related to the prehistoric culture in northwest China? These are our focuses. If there were connections, the best connection was the Yellow River.

In 2007, we conducted an on-site research and interviewed the leadership members in Taosi village. Why was this place determined to be the Yao capital by the archaeological authority? It was mainly because the Yao and Shun mythology was widespread there. More importantly, there was a Yao Temple (see Fig. 5.3). Renovated in the Qing dynasty, it should have been built earlier than that. In other words, our ancestors commemorated Yao here. Today, the Yao Temple is a tourist attraction and a must-go place for tourist groups. Here close to the Yao Temple, a city and graves 4,000 years ago were unearthed. Especially, there were the remains of an observatory, which

Fig. 5.3 Yao Temple at Xiangfen, Shanxi

archaeologists think represented the rising of imperial power in the Central Plain. Taosi was dated between 2300 B.C. to 1900 B.C. If it belonged to a dynasty, that dynasty was about 400 years old. How many years were Yao and Shun at the throne combined? Among the Chinese emperors, Qianlong was in office for 60 years. His reign was the longest. It is said that Yao sat on the throne for 70 years. Can you believe it? Zhu Xi conducted textual research and claimed that Yao's reign was 60 years, and after he retired, he continued to observe the world for 28 years. Combined, Yao lived for over 100 years. Obviously, that is a myth. The Yaosi era lasted around 400 years, which can be the lifespan of a dynasty. But the combined duration of the legendary Yao and Shun eras was merely several decades. So there was a huge gap between history and archaeology, and we need to continue our discussion and search for new evidence.

Among the narratives and texts about Yao and Shun that we discussed just now, we can sort out the issue about "瑞" (*rui*, jade ware). What is 辑五瑞 (gather five *rui*) and 班瑞于群后 (*ban rui yu qun hou*)? Five *rui* means five pieces of jade implements. They can serve as the agreement between man and gods. In the Holy Bible, the Old and New Testaments refer to the agreement between man and God, which were written on paper. In China, making an agreement with God does not require writing; holding a holy object would suffice. In the Zhou dynasty, the jade ritual objects refer to six different shapes with different meanings: *bi*, *cong*, *gui*, *hu*, *zhang* and *huang*.

Fig. 5.4 Origin of the Zhou ritual: holding the *bi* and *gui*. The white implement on the right is the earliest known jade *gui* unearthed in Taosi

5 Sages Yao and Shun: Chinese Sage Myths

The earliest *gui* unearthed in China was from the Taosi culture (see Fig. 5.4). Other people think that *gui* was shaped after the jade ax and jade shovel.

From this picture, we can tell that *gui* indeed existed over 4,000 years ago. Jade ritual objects' names were recorded in the literature of the Western Zhou dynasty, but they were not invented then. Western Zhou came into existed only some 3,000 years ago but the jade *gui* was from prehistoric culture. Once the prehistoric jade *gui* was unearthed, people knew that the objects described in *Rites of Zhou* were not fabricated. Most of them had a very long history. The two pieces of jade implements shown in Fig. 5.4 are pretty rare. They were unearthed by Shanxi Working team, Institute of Archaeology, Chinese Academy of Social Sciences, stored in the Institute's warehouse in Wangfujing in Beijing and were only shown on the 60th anniversary of the People's Republic of China. We call such jade ritual objects the fourth tier of evidence, the part that most deserves our attention.

Among the six jade ritual objects, the jade *bi* was usually used together with the jade *gui*. Especially in the early literature of the Western Zhou dynasty, *gui* and *bi* often appeared together. *Bi*, because of the story of "the return of the intact *bi* to Zhao," is known by most educated Chinese. This story happened during the Warring States period, over 2,000 years ago. Another piece of jade *bi* is 4,300 years old (see Fig. 5.5), twice as old as the Heshibi (the jade *bi* featured in the story of "the return of the intact *bi* to Zhao"). Shown in Shanxi Museum, it is the best in quality among the *bi* pieces unearthed in Taosi site. If you know how to appreciate jade, you can take a look at its quality. Though it had been buried underground for over 4,000 years, it looked like new when unearthed. The cotton fiber structure in the jade was very

Fig. 5.5 Jade *bi*, 4,300 years old, unearthed in Taosi, photographed in Shanxi Museum

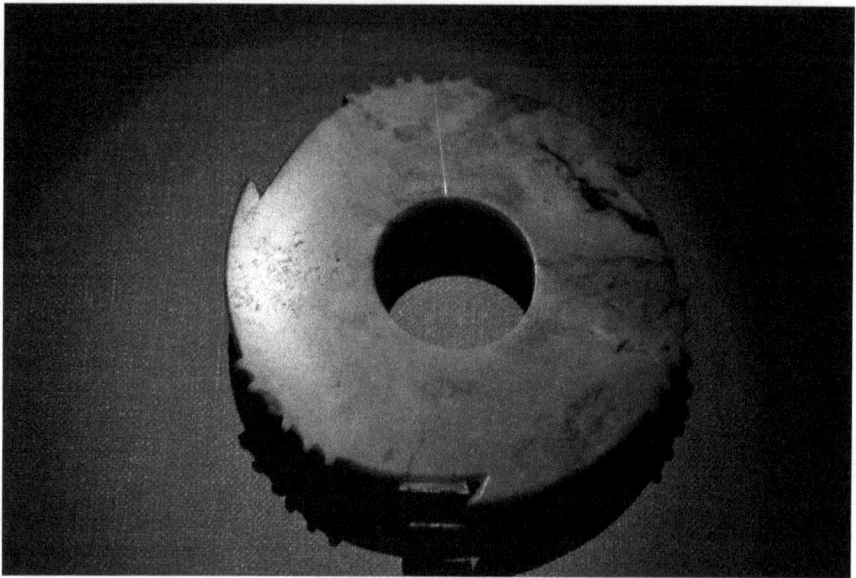

Fig. 5.6 Jade *Xuanji* unearthed in Taosi (Shanxi Museum)

obvious. Some people think it was Hetian jade, as the jade cotton structure was most visible in Hetian jade and not so in other kinds of jade.

As such good jade *bi* was unearthed in Taosi, we couldn't doubt that the cultural center of the Yao and Shun era wasn't here. We can't prove the existence or non-existence of Yao and Shun, but it is a fact that the rite system had been in existence in that era. Our explanation to 璇玑玉衡 *xuan ji yu heng*[2] was too brief just now. A pretty authoritative archaeologist thinks that it was not *xuanji* the astronomical observation device, but a jade *bi* with teeth. He named it "teeth *bi*" (see Fig. 5.6) but we do not agree with this. It is indeed a jade *bi*, but in a spiral shape with gear-like structures. Actually, these details are symbols to tell people that this piece of bi was specially produced.

Common tools for utilitarian purposes would not have been carved with these gears. It was a holy ritual object. In ancient times, to achieve the unity of heaven and man and to observe the celestial phenomena, it was quite possible that our ancestors used jade or bronze to make measurement tools. The jade *xuanji* of Taosi solidly proved that the *Canon of Yao* was not groundless in telling that people of the Yao and Shun era planned their farming activities based on observations of celestial phenomena.

Rui as explained by *Shuowen Jiezi* was "jade as a contract". The contract is binding not only between humans, but humans and gods. If you ask me which binding relationship was more important, my answer is definitely the one between humans and gods. Humans' credibility comes from the celestial gods and beliefs. The *Rites of*

---

[2]Translator's note: It's meaning is explained in the following paragraphs.

5 Sages Yao and Shun: Chinese Sage Myths

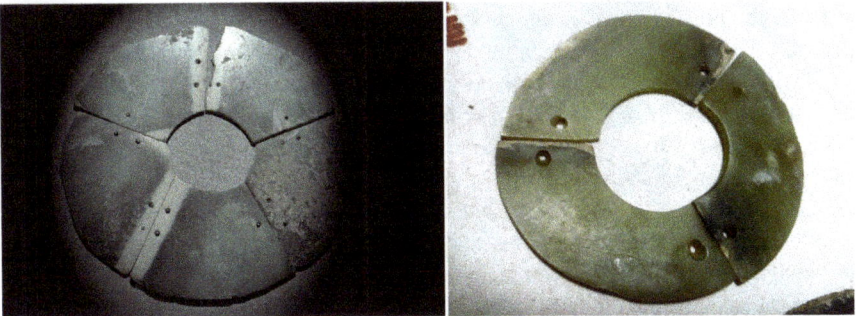

Fig. 5.7 Jade *bi* formed by multiple pieces of *huang*

Zhou said, "掌玉瑞器之藏", and the annotation was "the jade implement is something people hold as tokens, symbols and contract." When political groups are trying to get along, they need jade implements to establish good relationships. Jade *rui* is the token of an alliance. If one side does not have it, conflicts or wars might occur. As a token from gods to humans selected in the prehistoric era, the jade *rui* was actually *gui*, according to the *Book of Rites*. When the ministers went to the court, they each held a board in their hands. That board was transformed from the jade *gui*. The original meaning of *rui* 瑞 can be found in some words, such as *ruigui* (瑞珪, a *gui* jade granted by the emperor as a token), *ruijie* (瑞节, a jade token), *ruiling* (瑞令, the manifest destiny bestowed by heaven to the emperor), and *ruiyu* (瑞玉, jade token). Its extended meaning is "auspicious things or signs." As *Lunheng* goes, "the world call it the auspicious sign of a sage king 世间谓之圣王之瑞." A quotation from *Mozi*: "Yu held the heaven's auspicious order in hand to declare war against the Youmiao clan. 禹亲把天之瑞令, 以征有苗." Only after the god gave Yu this order did he have the right to fight and kill. There is what *banrui* 班瑞 meant: distributing jade. After the emperor's reign was established during the Yao and Shun era, how was the local power managed? The emperor gave each local leader a piece of jade. Together those pieces form a complete piece of jade; separated, they were called the jade *huang*. Jade *bi* formed by multiple pieces of *huang* is only found from the middle to upper reaches of the Yellow River. Jade culture was found at the lower reaches of the Yangtze River as early as 5,000 years ago, but no such kind of jade was founded. The jade *bi* formed by multiple pieces of *huang* unearthed in Taosi clearly showed that people at that time did not rely on personal connections to recognize alliance, but the token jade. Some *bi* was formed by five pieces of *huang*, some three, and some two, which was the least (see Fig. 5.7). Distributed, each piece is given to each subordinate; combined, the pieces form common sovereignty.

The above demonstrated how we used the latest archaeological discoveries such as the jade ritual objects from Taosi to examine which parts of the *Canon of Yao* from *The Book of Documents* were credible.

As to proving false, modern scholars have stopped believing in the legend of abdication of the crown, so I will spare my effort here. More importantly, we discovered the social features 4,000 years ago at Taosi: it was a violent era. Here I quote a paper titled "On Yao and Shun's Abdication and Usurping of the Crown 也谈尧舜禅让与篡夺" which was included in a collection of papers, *Research of the Xiangfen Taosi Site* (2007) 襄汾陶寺遗址研究. This collection contained archaeologists' findings. Through the discoveries of tombs and palaces, they showed that it was not a peaceful society back then. First, the city walls of the middle Taosi era were overlaid or broken in the later era and the city was breached and then rebuilt, meaning that wars took place there. Second, the ruined constructions of the middle Taosi era were covered by garbage from the late Taosi era. Palace turning into a garbage dump, it meant that the palace was abandoned. Third, dozens of headless bodies filled an ash pit, most of whom were youths or middle-aged. That was a horrifying scene. Fourth, a female skeleton of about 35 years old had her neck broken and had an ox horn plugged in her vagina. Archaeologists used it as irrefutable evidence of the violent abuse of enemy's women. Fifth, objects from the late Taosi culture was found to have pressed on the sacrifice zone of the small cities in the mid-era, which meant that the latecomers overthrew the previous generations' temples. Sixth, bones of the tomb owner in coffin M8 were destroyed and misplaced, and in the pit under coffin M22 scattered five human skulls. With these pieces of evidence only, it was still difficult to draw any conclusion for lacking comparison. 5,000–6,000 years ago, before the Taosi culture, Yangshao culture was at the central plain. Surrounding the settlement was only the entrenchment to fend against animals and no high city walls could be found. It was obvious that it was a relatively peaceful era. Anthony Giddens, the British sociologist, expressed his idea that the nation-state is built on violence, including prison, police and the army, in his representative book titled *The Nation-state and Violence*. Therefore, Taosi represented one of the earliest urban civilizations in the

Fig. 5.8 Jade implements in Shimao site (Shaanxi Shenmu Museum)

Central Plain. In that social environment, was it possible for a retiring king to look for a farmer in the field as his successor? It was very unlikely.

Except the Taosi site, hundreds of kilometers away on the west bank of the Yellow River, close to the Hetao region in the north, people discovered a huge city site. That was the most impressive Shimao site. Archaeologists started the official research of the Shimao site in Shenmu Town in 2011 and released a brief in 2012: they discovered the largest city of the prehistoric China. Taosi of 2.8 million square meters was pretty big, but the Shimao city was over 4 million square meters, much larger than the former. Here, many jade ritual objects were unearthed too, which were dated 4,300 to 1,900 years ago. These are the jade implements on display in Shenmu Museum (see Fig. 5.8).

Fig. 5.9 A map of the distribution of the Longshan culture in Shaanxi, Shaanxi History Museum

If you wonder where Shenmu is, it is along the Yellow River at the side of Shaanxi province. Going through central Shaanxi is a grand river, the largest branch of the Yellow River. That is River Wei, as appeared in the four-character set phrase "泾渭分明" (as distinct from each other as the two rivers Jing and Wei). South to River Wei was Qinling Mountains. Shaanxi History Museum displayed the distribution

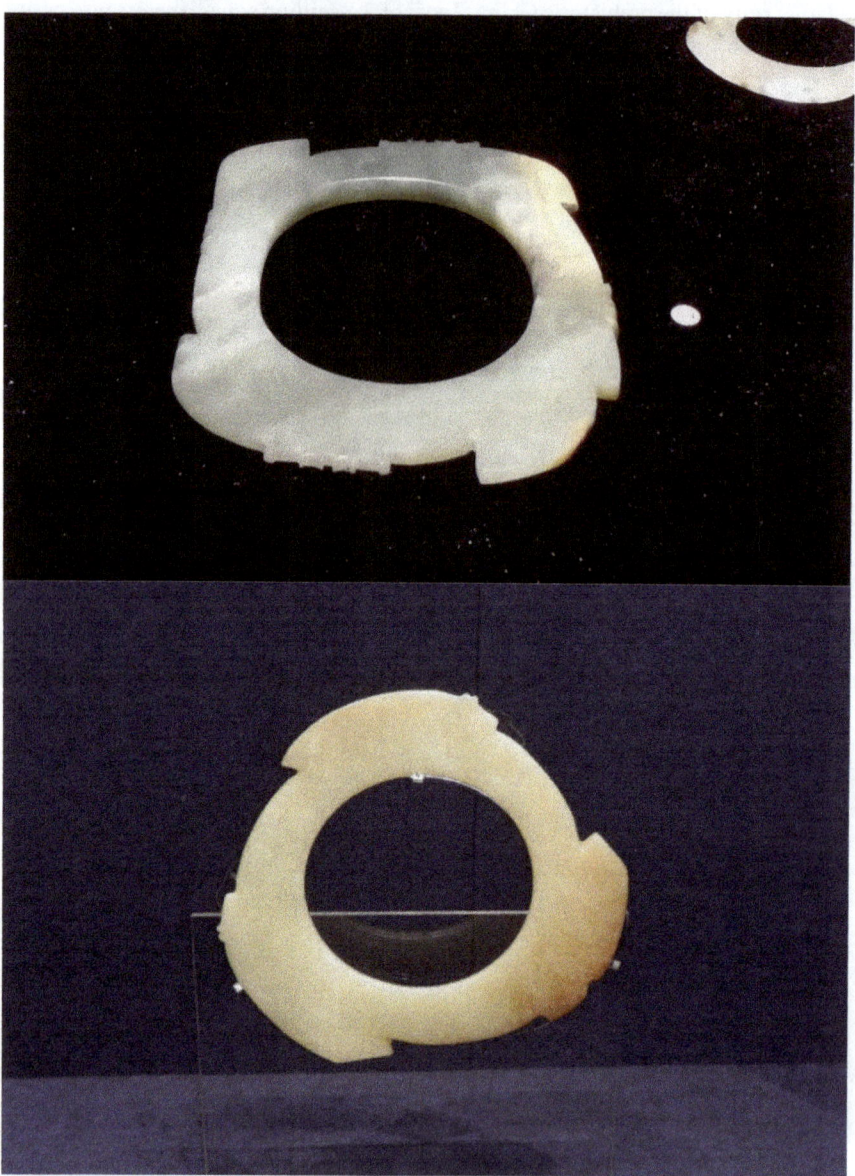

Fig. 5.10 Jade *xuanji* unearthed in the old city of Shimao

of the prehistoric sites in Shaanxi over 4,000 years ago. Please take a look at the distribution map of Longshan Culture in Shaanxi (see Fig. 5.9). What surprises us is its difference from today's Shaanxi. Today, Shaanxi's Guanzhong Plain is abundant and rich, while north and south Shaanxi is poorer with fewer resources. But according to the ruins from 4,000 years ago, the cultural sites were mostly in north Shaanxi area with relatively fewer in Guanzhong. How come were these ruins from Longshan culture over 4,000 years ago so densely distributed in north Shaanxi? It reflects a huge mismatch between the macro tradition and micro tradition.

The Shimao ruins of Shenmu town was close to north Shaanxi. There was the jade *xuanji* that we just mentioned (see Fig. 5.10). The jade *xuanji* could only be found in the Yellow River region in China, which meant that there was the inheritance of a unified jade culture behind the establishment of the northern sovereignty. Though there were many pieces of jade implements in Shimao, it was estimated that around 4,000–5,000 pieces were missing in the contemporary era. Today in Shaanxi History Museum there is a display counter, which lays a piece of dark jade implement that is over one *chi* long (around 30 cm). The sheer volume of material used is indeed very impressive. Both the jade *zhang* and jade spade could be considered weapons and ritual implements with blades (see Fig. 5.11). Why were they mass-produced and used then? What did they represent? They are the best physical evidence that we can find about an era as early as the Xia dynasty. Also, the jade broadsword with holes can be found in the Yellow River region and the Yangtze River region (see Fig. 5.12).

In Anhui Provincial Museum at Hefei, Anhui, a gigantic jade broadsword is displayed, which is shaped very similarly with the jade broadsword with holes. Were the many unearthed jade broadswords used for cutting or for rituals? Today opinions mostly lean towards the latter, since in Shenmu people have discovered another ruins site called Xinhua. In its sacrifice pit were 36 pieces of jade implements inserted in the ground, in lines with birds' bodies scattered among them. It was obviously from a sacrifice ceremony to heaven. These were the intermediaries between the gods and people.

The below table (Table 5.1) chronologizes the mythologies related to jade implements in Chinese culture, starting from the era when they first appeared and ending with Emperor Qin using the jade heirloom seal to symbolize the unified empire. It seems that the symbol of the Han China's sovereignty remained the same from 211 B.C. through 1911. Before the jade seal, many other jade ritual objects were treated as power symbols. In the past, people didn't know if these legends were true or not. Now as we see them, they should all be true, because they had all been unearthed, accompanied by a large number of nameless jade objects. The complexity of the jade ritual has gone beyond the written record. Words are like the sieve. Those remain on the sieve were passed down, but those that went through were forgotten. If we want to find out the reality about the era of Yao and Shun, we should shift our focus from Confucianism and Mohism discourses to the relics with over 4,000 years of history. This chronology presents a pretty complete list of kings and rulers' narratives in history about jade rituals, which can be validated.

With this chronology, a question ensued: neither Shanxi nor north Shaanxi had any jade mines, where did the jade material come from in the prehistoric era in

Fig. 5.11 Jade *zhang* and jade spade from Shimao, Shaanxi History Museum

5 Sages Yao and Shun: Chinese Sage Myths

Fig. 5.12 Jade broadswords with holes, sacrifice objects from Shimao, Shaanxi History Museum

Table 5.1 Chinese chronology in macro tradition governed by the jade belief system

Jade mythology 1	Jade snake: jade *jue* and jade ax	8,000 years ago
Jade mythology 2	Rainbow dragon: jade *huang* and jade *ben*	7,000 years ago
Jade mythology 3	Royal power: jade *yue* and jade *gui*	6,000 years ago
Jade mythology 4	Yellow Emperor eating jade: jade *ying* and jade *bi*	5,000 years ago
Jade mythology 5	Yao and Shun holding the jade: jade *zhang* and jade *ge*	4,300 years ago
Jade mythology 6	Xia Yu Xuangui; gold and jade ritual implement set	4,000 years ago
Jade mythology 7	King Zhou of Shang and his Heaven Wisdom Jade	3,200 years ago
Jade mythology 8	Jiang Ziya fishing jade *huang*	3,000 years ago
Jade mythology 9	King Mu of Zhou visiting jade on Kunlun Mountain	2,800 years ago
Jade mythology 10	King Chu getting the Heshibi jade	2,500 years ago
Jade mythology 11	King Zhao of Qin requesting the Heshibi	2,300 years ago
Jade mythology 12	First Emperor Qin's Heirloom Seal of the Realm	2,200 years ago

Note This table is from *A Mythological Research of the Sources of the Chinese Civilization*, Social Sciences Literature Press, 2015

the east and west bank of the Yellow River? Was it from the Kunlun Mountain in Xinjiang? Thousands of kilometers away from the Central Plain, was it possible to transport jade from Xinjiang? The Literary Anthropology Society conducted ten field trips, and one of the main goals was to figure out the source of jade. One thing is certain: the jade used in ancient Central Plain states was mainly from the west. The *Classic of Mountains and Seas* mentioned that the Kunlun Mountain was called the Jade Mountain, and Queen Mother of the West lived in Yaochi, the Jade Pool. Both places were associated with jade. We just discussed that according to *Guanzi*, Yao and Shun's secret to establishing sovereignty was "北用禺氏之玉", using jade from the Yu clan in the north. Though Yao and Shun's sovereignty was established in the Central Plain, the jade used to symbolize their royal power was from the north. It might not have come from the north, but the west in Inner Mongolia. If we juxtapose the jade from the Kunlun Mountain, and the jade ritual object cultural cluster of over 4,000 years old in the middle reaches of the Yellow River, we can tell that most of the jade used were not produced locally, especially those Hetian jade objects that we just saw. Nowhere in the east of Qinghai did we find jade of such good quality, let alone in Shanxi. Therefore, we need to look for the routes to transport jade. Record about such routes in Yao and Shun's era was just one sentence from *Guanzi*, but in the era of King Mu of Zhou, a complete narrative about the jade transportation from the west to the east can be found in the *Tale of King Mu, Son of Heaven*. It recorded that rulers of the Western Zhou left the Central Plain for Kunlun Mountain. In name, they were to visit the Queen Mother of the West, but in fact, they were to collect the Hetian jade. *The Tale of King Mu, Son of Heaven* contains four characters: 载玉万只 (carry tens of thousands pieces of jade). After the Western Zhou dynasty, the Jade Road was in operation. Unexpectedly, the Jade Road did not follow the route of the Silk Road from Luoyang, Xi'an to Tianshui and Lanzhou. Instead, it mainly followed along the Yellow River and its branches. In ancient times, no route was in existence, except the road walked by King Mu of Zhou. First, one would cross the Yellow River to arrive at Shanxi, pass Yanmenguan and arrive at Hetao, then go west along the Yellow River. As ancient people believed that the Yellow River originated from the Kunlun Mountain, as they said, "The River comes from Kunlun 河出昆仑." Their descendants firmly believed that the Kunlun Mountain is the source of both the beautiful jade and the Central Plain people's drinking water.

The route of Hexi Corridor was formed around 4,000 years ago. Was there an even earlier road? Yes, but with sporadic cultural exchanges, those roads bore little meaning. Around 4,000 years ago, culture began to spread. Many important elements in the Han Chinese culture were brought in from Hexi Corridor that was opened 4,000 years ago. The foremost was the gold. The Chinese have attached equal importance to the gold and the jade. The Central Plain didn't have gold in the first place. The first gold object in China was unearthed in Yumen City of the Hexi Corridor region. That place was called the Huoshaogou Relic Site. Now we know where the gold came from. It came from West Asia, Central Asia and Xinjiang along the Hexi Corridor. The nomadic people especially liked gold objects, so the biggest difference between the Huns and the Han Chinese, according to the *Records of the Grand Historian*, was that the Han Chinese liked jade. While Emperor Qin Shihuang only

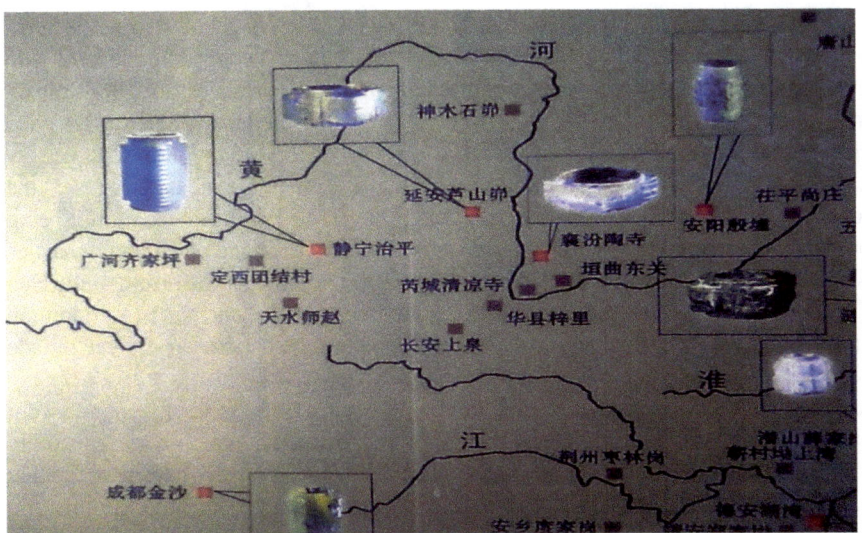

Fig. 5.13 A distribution map of the jade *cong*, produced by the Liangzhu Museum, Hangzhou, Zhejiang

used jade objects to represent his power and unification, the Huns used golden figures as sacrifices to the sky. Today we have discovered a large amount of precious metal in grassland culture. The spread of precious metal was related to Hexi Corridor. Another example is the wheat we eat. Wheat wasn't found in other relic sites except in Longshan Cultural sites. The era around 4,000 years ago was very memorable; because it was then that the Hexi Corridor was open for traffic. The earliest wheat cultivation was found in the area from Palestine to Turkey, around 12,000 years ago. China's wheat appeared 8,000 years later. During the 8,000 years, wheat spread east from the heart of Eurasia, like the domino. It goes without saying that Hexi Corridor is crucial to our understanding of the Chinese culture.

Through the thread of jade ritual implements in Yao and Shun's era, we connect the upper and middle reaches of the Yellow River. In the past, when we examined the questions related to Yao and Shun, we focused on the Central Plain, either south Shanxi or West Henan. We were fixated on finding evidence to prove the existence of the earliest sovereignty of Xia, Shang and Zhou dynasties in these places. Now as we see it, archaeological discoveries have corrected our prejudice that only the Central Plain could be the focus. We have witnessed how the Northwestern prehistoric culture that goes along the Yellow River influenced the culture in the Central Plain. Liangzhu Museum produced this distribution map of the jade *cong* (see Fig. 5.13). Jade *cong* was invented in the prehistoric civilization in the South by people living in the Taihu Lake region to the Hangzhou Bay. Around 4,000 years ago, the jade *cong* had unified China's northern area. According to the marked places where 4,000-year-old *cong* were unearthed, we can roughly guess that the influence came along the Yellow River.

It was not only unpractical to make a piece of jade *cong* but also wasteful in material. What an unbelievable achievement to produce such a large piece of jade implement with a round hole in the middle! Why did our ancestors go all out to make that? A saying goes that the heaven is round and the land is square. The jade *cong*, square at the outside and round at the inside, represents deity's power. Its actual function was to connect heaven and earth. It was a holy object to represent the royal power. After the Western Zhou dynasty, the jade *cong* disappeared, not being produced nor used. Only from the prehistoric era to Xia, Shang and Zhou dynasties was the jade *cong* used as ritual objects. As long as we consider the origin of the Han Chinese civilization and the prehistoric culture that used the jade *cong* as a common entity under the jade ritual culture, the situation will become clearer. A piece of jade *cong* unearthed in Jingning town was placed in Gansu Museum. It was a very big model and the jade used was of high quality. Obviously, it was the green jade from Hetian (see Fig. 5.14). This piece also bore groove pattern, which was exquisitely grinded. It represented the highest technology then, as it was very hard to make that pattern. Four thousand years ago, the jade *cong* was mass produced in prehistoric culture, including the Taosi culture. It means that the prehistoric civilization from the upper to the middle reaches of the Yellow River was connected. The jade *bi* was very common in Gansu, because Gansu was the closest with where the raw jade material was produced. The convenient access to raw material made Gansu home to much more pieces of jade ritual objects than the Central Plain region. Zhongfu Museum at Dingxi, Gansu is a private museum. The curator has collected hundreds of pieces of jade *huang* (see Fig. 5.15), much more than those in a national museum.

Through the question about the transportation route of jade, we consider Xinjiang and the Central Plain as a common cultural entity. The resource was in Xinjiang, while the consumers were in the Central Plain. Local people in Xinjiang didn't use jade, as the ethnic minority groups didn't have the jade ritual tradition. To them, the jade is no different from the stone. But the Han Chinese living thousands of *li* away thought Xinjiang had the best jade, so they spared no effort getting through this route in the hope to continuously transport Xinjiang jade to the Central Plain. The Silk Road was coined by a German named Ferdinand von Richtofen in 1877. Only after the Opium War were foreigners allowed to enter China. Among the earliest were geologists, scholars and historians. Westerners didn't produce silk, so the price of silk was ten times that of gold. They didn't know where the silk came from except that it was from the East. The German geographer Ferdinand von Richthofen traveled to the Hexi Corridor and found that Xinjiang was connected to Central Plain and Middle Asia, which was further connected to the Mediterranean. Therefore, he called this route the Silk Road. When was this road opened? This German considered the Silk Road officially opened in 138 B.C., when Zhang Qian paid visits to China's neighbors in the West, as recorded in Sima Qian's *Records of the Grand Historian*. It was over 2,100 years ago. I would say that the China portion of the Silk Road was already in use 4,000 years ago and was in full operation 2,000 years ago.

When the Chinese culture began to form, two important events marked the cultural communication back then. One was the spread of the jade culture from the east to the west, and the other was the transportation of jade from the west to the east. We

Fig. 5.14 Jade *cong* unearthed in Jingning, Qijia culture (2000 B.C.), collected by Gansu Provincial Museum

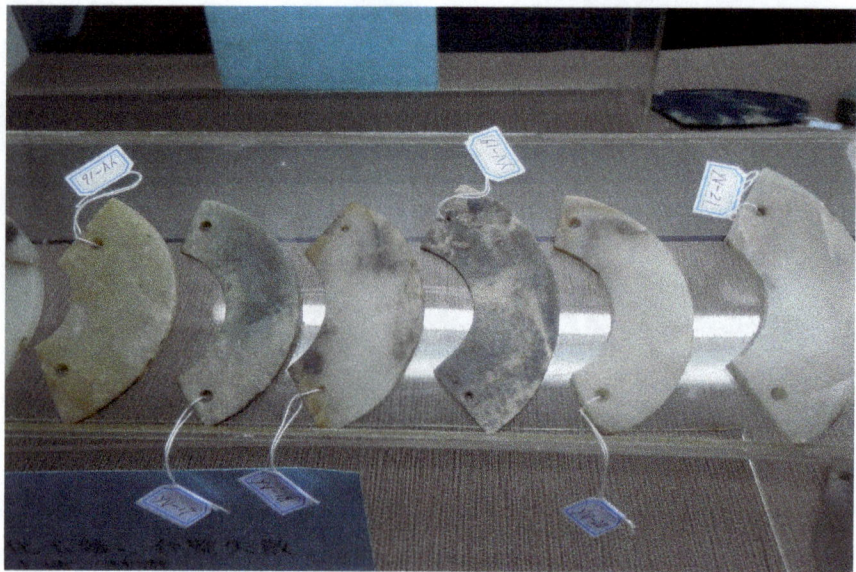

Fig. 5.15 Jade *huang* of Qijia culture, Zhongfu Museum, Dingxi, Gansu

can provide a relatively reasonable answer to the question of why jade was used as tokens and ritual objects during the Yao and Shun's era. The spread of the jade culture from the east to the west means that the jade culture originated in Chifeng region in Northeast China 8,000 years ago. It spread from the north along the eastern coastal areas to Guangdong, Taiwan and Vietnam. East China was firstly influenced by jade culture, before the Central Plain and West China. This process was called the spread of the jade culture from the east to the west. Jade culture appeared in Northeast China 8,000 years ago, and didn't reach Wuwei, Gansu, which was the mid Hexi Corridor region, until 4,000 years ago. The spread of jade culture took thousands of years. More importantly, once jade culture reached Hexi Corridor, which connected Xinjiang, the best jade material entered. In the prehistoric era, almost all the jade used in production was locally excavated. After the Xia, Shang and Zhou dynasties, when the high-quality jade from the west came, the price of local jade plummeted; because jade was used only by the rulers, who only recognized the jade from Kunlun Mountain in Xinjiang as the best. The jade ritual objects by those in power were made by professional jade craftsmen, who could easily distinguish the good material from the bad. This transportation route of jade from the west to the east started operation around 4,000 years ago during the Qijia Culture, which was twice as early compared to the time judged by the German geographer Richthofen.

What was transported earlier was the jade from the east of the Hexi Corridor, not from the west of the Corridor. We discovered several ancient jade mine zones in the east of the Corridor. It has been about 4,000 years since Xinjiang jade entered the Central Plain, and about 5,000 years since Gansu started transporting jade. Now we have figured out the two stages in China's jade cultural history. One was the jade ritual culture. People worshiped and believed in jade. They thought that jade represents deities, so they mass produced and used jade ritual objects. Next, Hetian jade was selected and recognized as the best jade material. In today's market, the jade from Xiuyan, Liaoning is about RMB ¥10 per *jin* (500 grams). Meanwhile, Hetian nephrite white jade is RMB ¥20,000 per gram. The vast difference in price was not caused by any individual, but by 4,000 years of cultural tradition.

After Taosi was Shimao culture at the west bank of the Yellow River. The prehistoric walls and constructions found locally were exquisite, which were built with local stones. People were farming under the city wall when archaeologists recognized the ancient remains. When asked what that was, they answered that it was the Great Wall. North Shaanxi was indeed within the area covered by the Great Wall from Qin and Han dynasties. There was also the Ming Great Wall. Local people had no idea which dynasty the Wall belonged to. In 2011, an archaeologist team came for research. They took the wood materials in the stone cracks to do carbon-14 testing. When the result came out, everyone was surprised. The Shimao city was 4,000 to 4,300 years old. This city was well designed: an outer city, an inner city and a barbican. Outside the city wall was a half circle. When enemies came in, you just need to close the gates of the barbican and kill off those invaders on the wall, just like catching the turtle in a jar. The city wall 4,000 years ago has every defense mechanism we know today. This city is indeed an astonishing archaeological discovery. It used stone and earth as bricks and wood as reinforcement. But one thing to our surprise was that between stones were jade objects. That was unexpected (see Fig. 5.16). This city was very grand. On a sunny day, one is able to see it standing on a higher place on the Shanbei Plateau dozens of kilometers away. Built against the hillside, the outer city and inner city guarded the crown 4,000 years ago. The city wall was several meters in width at some points, which meant an enormous amount of work.

Emperor Qin Shihuang conquered all the lands of China but wasn't able to maintain his power. The Qin dynasty just lasted a dozen years. The reason, as reflected from the story of "Lady Meng Jiang weeps the Great Wall", was that Emperor Qin Shihuang requisitioned all the labor force in China, so the national power declined. How much labor was used in building such a large city as the Shimao City?

Nowadays, this place has little population. We have no idea what it was like 4,000 years ago. At the east gate of the city was a gable. After it collapsed, people discovered six pieces of jade objects between the rocks (Fig. 5.17). The jade objects were inserted when the city was built in the first place. That is quite hard to comprehend. The legend goes that Emperor Jie of Xia built 瑶台 and 玉门 (jade terrace and jade gates), but nobody knew what exactly they looked like. Today we see this rock gate wall with jade objects inserted, and it is very likely to be the legendary structure. The jade material in our new discoveries in Shimao is similar to Hetian jade, most of which seemed to be from Gansu, coming along the Yellow River and its branches.

There was another astonishing discovery in Shimao relic site: a massive human skull sacrifice offerings. In 2012, a pit containing 24 human skulls were discovered. When building a city, people had to seek forgiveness by offering sacrifices or jade once they broke the ground. Similarly, people from some ethnic minority groups pay

Fig. 5.16 Prehistoric city wall in Shimao at the west bank of the Yellow River 4,000 years ago

5 Sages Yao and Shun: Chinese Sage Myths

Fig. 5.17 Six pieces of jade objects unearthed in Shimao

respect to the earth with silver coins or jade objects nowadays. The 24 skulls found in Shimao were all young females. It means that a patriarchal society had formed so they used females as sacrifices. In April 2013, China Literary Anthropology Society and China Association of Collectors held a conference themed "China Jade Road and Jade Weapon Culture" in Shimao. Many jade objects unearthed here were like weapons, as they had blades. How come they appear here in cluster? Where did the jade come from? To answer these questions, we invited experts to share their opinions in the conference. *The Formation of China Based on the Jade Culture* 玉成中国 was the collection of papers from this conference. The main question of the research was the transportation route of the west jade to the Central Plain. A young director from CCTV (China Central Television) recorded the whole conference, and made a documentary called *Shimao the Ancient Town* 石破天惊石峁古城. If you want to know what China was like 4,000 years ago, it should be the latest live teaching material. The first two episodes were about the Shimao relic site, and the latter two episodes were about the jade implements in Shimao.

After this conference, we launched a very extensive and in-depth research on the route of the Jade Road. Started in Yanmenguan in Shanxi, we studied the two sides of Hetao region and Hexi Corridor to the Westmost point of Xinjiang, covering seven to eight provinces and around 200 towns and cities in West China. We stopped at the places that produced jade or had ancient jade ritual and took samples, photos, or wrote reports. Through this systematic research, we had an idea when and through which route the west of the Central Plain was accessible. We also proposed the theory

Fig. 5.18 Jade *cong* unearthed in Shaoguan, Guangdong, 4,000 years old

Fig. 5.19 Jade *cong* unearthed from the area on the east of the Hexi Corridor, Dingxi Museum

that jade culture united China from the very beginning. Based on the distribution of jade ritual objects around 4,000 years ago, we decided that this culture spread in a way that was similar to the spread of a religion. Where did the belief in jade come from? Around 8,000 years ago, the jade ritual culture in North China was like sparks of fire that kept spreading. Fast forward 4,000 years, this culture arrived at the Pearl River region in Guangdong, covering most parts of China except the Tibetan Plateau and Xinjiang. Now I am going to talk about three pieces of jade *cong*. One is 4,000 years old that was unearthed in Shaoguan, Guangdong (see Fig. 5.18), one was from the area on the east of the Hexi Corridor (see Fig. 5.19) and the third one, a long piece, was recently unearthed from the Jinsha relic site of today's Chengdu (see Fig. 5.20). The discovery of these objects indicates that jade ritual culture had been spreading all over China. Such rituals formed the jade ritual culture of the Xia, Shang and Zhou as we know now. Confucius once sighed: Is ritual merely reflected on jade and silk! 礼云礼云, 玉帛云乎哉! Without jade, our ancestors' ritual would be like a team without a leader. The 33 cm-long large piece of jade implement, or the

Fig. 5.20 Jade *cong* unearthed in Jinsha Site, Chengdu

4,000-year-old tooth-shaped *zhang* can basically be found throughout China from north to south (see Fig. 5.21). This indicates that the jade ritual culture spread widely just like religions. Yao and Shun's era must have grown and thrived from the jade ritual culture.

We have discussed two archaeological sites among the three. The last one is the Lajia site. It was also discovered in the 21st century, in Lajia village of Minhe, Qinghai. Home to ethnic minority groups, the village is by the Yellow River (see Fig. 5.22). The Shimao site that we just saw stood closely to the Yellow River along its branch, and so was the Lajia site. From archaeological studies, people concluded that the prehistoric culture was drowned by the Yellow River when it flooded. Lajia

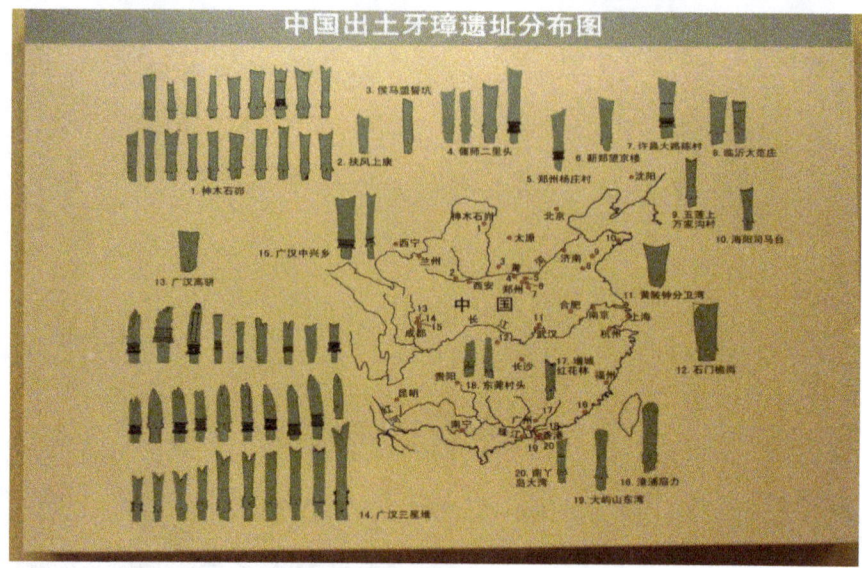

Fig. 5.21 A distribution map of sites where tooth-shaped *zhang* was unearthed in China, Shaanxi History Museum

Fig. 5.22 Lajia village

5 Sages Yao and Shun: Chinese Sage Myths 133

Fig. 5.23 Jade broadsword with holes (Qinghai Museum)

Village had been a small village in the remote area of Qinghai province. In the beginning of the 21st century, a group of archaeologists stopped here for a rest, and saw some kids rolling an iron hoop. A closer look, they found the hoop was not made of iron, but jade, and this jade hoop was not new, but from thousands of years ago. They asked the villagers where it came from, and the answer was that they often dig out jade objects like this in the field. Thus, a prehistoric cultural site was found here. It belonged to the Qijia culture, which was widely distributed in Gansu and Qinghai. The Lajia site is one of the most important historical sites in Qinghai region so far. Opposite to the Yellow River was the Jishi Mountain, which was said to be the starting point of Yu in his endeavor to curb the flood. The expression in historical record was "dredge the River [from] Jishi 导河积石." The River is the Yellow River. When Yu was fighting the flood, one side of the River was Gansu, and the other side was Qinghai. At Dahejia Port, we saw the surprising aspect of the Lajia site: the mass-produced jade ritual objects unearthed here were basically the same as those from Shimao. They were in geometric shapes without any carved decoration. The jade broadsword displayed in Qinghai Museum (see Fig. 5.23) was also unearthed here. The longest was 60 to 70 cm. To make it, one needed a huge piece of jade material. Why on earth did the ancient people put efforts in it?

Through the Lajia site, we have a rough idea about the Qijia culture in the west. Existed 4,100 years ago to 3,500 years ago, Qijia culture lasted approximately 600 years. Its most distinctive feature was the mass production and use of jade ritual objects. We guess that everyone back then wore a piece of jade, just like we carry our ID. Jade resource was abundant there. The newly discovered jade mine

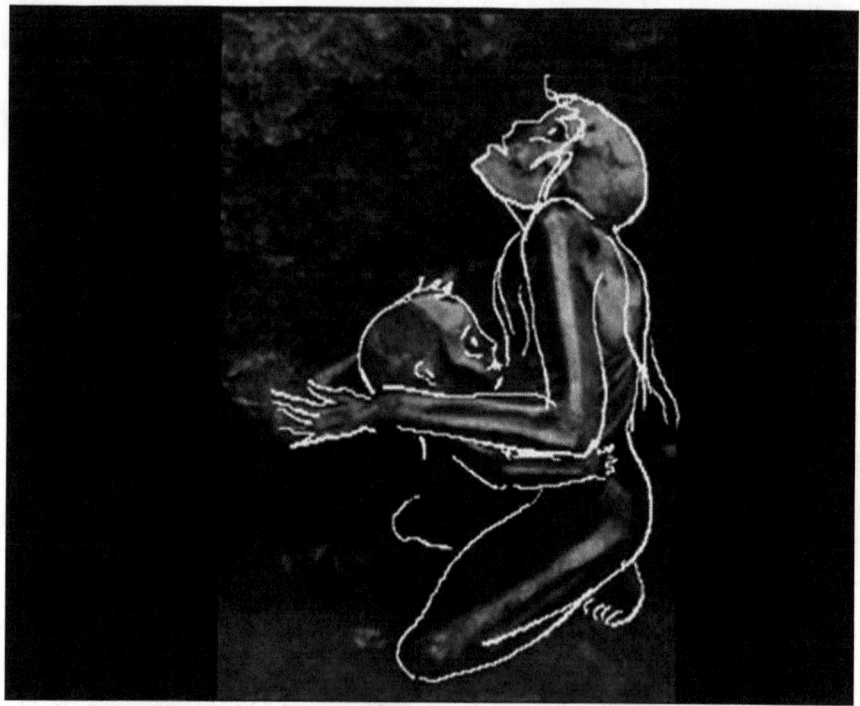

Fig. 5.24 Earthquake 4,000 years ago: Qinghai people and the Lajia relic site

in Gansu produced quality jade material that was similar to the Hetian jade, which we had no knowledge of before. The prehistoric jade ritual culture in northwest China was once prominent, and its distribution was very close to the territories of the Shang and Zhou dynasties. As for the origin of the Xia dynasty, the notion 大禹出西羌 (Great Yu was from the West Qiang region) repeated in ancient records. People from the Central Plain thought that people from the west did not grow grains because the Qiang people were shepherds. Half of the Han Chinese could find their ancestry from the Qiang people who entered the Central Plain. The notion "Great Yu was from the West Qiang region" was very important, as it indicated that the source of the Xia culture was relevant to the west. No written records existed for the prehistoric culture in the Northwest. Why did this culture cease to exist? The Lajia site provided a persuasive explanation, that is an 8.0-magnitude earthquake had occurred here. Back then, people lived in loess house caves that were the same as those lived by peasants in North Shaanxi today. During the earthquake, the cave dwelling collapsed. In this picture, we can see a mother trying to protect her child as the ceiling fell on them. With scanning technology, this skeleton shows a mother protecting her child during the earthquake (see Fig. 5.24).

Except the earthquake, the cave dwellings were threatened by floods as they were close to the Yellow River. Similarly, landslide dams also brought floods that destroyed

Fig. 5.25 The first bowl of noodle in the world

the cave dwellings. Qijia culture underwent the similar fate. Around 4,000 years ago, Qijia culture became prominent, but was destroyed by natural disasters around 3,500 to 3,600 years ago. Nobody saved them back then. Judging from the condition afterwards, epidemics and food shortage struck this place. If a prehistoric civilization was not able to withstand natural disasters, it was very likely to be wiped off from the map. The Lajia site showed us that in the upper Yellow River region, brilliant prehistoric culture existed 4,000 years ago, and its people must have relations with the Di and Qiang people. Fortunately, despite the natural disaster, everything was sealed intact thereby. Archaeologists found the "first bowl of noodles in the world," which made a Science cover story (see Fig. 5.25). The noodles were not made of wheat, but another kind of staple food, the *Mi* (or *Shu*). They were not much different from today's instant noodles by appearance. The noodle-loving northwestern Chinese was eating noodles 4,000 years ago! We have this solid evidence.

Around 4,000 years ago, a great change occurred again. A note for everyone: when transporting the best jade from West China to the east, people also brought precious metal, wheat and cotton. The biggest change happened to the prehistoric culture at Hexi Corridor after Qijia culture, was the arrival of the nomadic people on horseback, which bore great significance. In the ruins on the Central Plain before the Shang dynasty, not a piece of bone from the domestic horse was found. So, the horse was not cultivated locally. Where was it from? Please look at the map: it came from the western prairie. The best breed was the Akhal-Teke. When Emperor Wu of Han saw an Akhai-Teke horse after sending Zhang Qian as an envoy to the west, he had a poem written for this foreign breed. The poem was titled *Song*

Fig. 5.26 A couple's joint burial, Liuwan Museum of Ancient Painted Pottery

of the Heavenly Horse. Along with jade, the horse was a more important import from the Hexi Corridor. The Qin soldiers all relied on horse carts during wars. One cannot exaggerate horses' influence on the Han Chinese civilization. The Central Plain had never seen the horse, so the earliest horse was called the "long" (dragon). Ancient books such as *Erya* told people that "the horse of eight chi long is called the dragon 马八尺为龙." "Heavenly horse galloping across the sky" (天马行空 wildly imaginative) and "dragon and horse spirit" (龙马精神 good spirit) are both Chinese people's discourse and narratives with mythological overtone. Therefore, to describe this strain of civilization, the most suitable word was "mythistory".

The rise of Qijia Culture 4,000 years ago brought about another important change, that is the change in man and woman's status and power. In a village by the Xining-Lanzhou highway, there was a prehistoric tomb group. That is where the Liuwan Museum of Ancient Painted Pottery located. A Japanese once passed the tombs and couldn't bear to see so many pieces of antiques lying there, so he donated money to build the museum. There unearthed tens of thousand pieces of painted pottery objects, but only 500 were displayed in the museum. Before jade implements appeared, all the ritual objects in the Northwest China 5,000 years ago were made of clay. Here, the clay objects showed three colors. Some even bore the animal-shaped god images. A burial arrangement from the Qijia culture in Liuwan Museum of Ancient Painted Pottery can best illustrate the issue (see Fig. 5.26). A man lies inside a coffin carved from a whole piece of wood, and two females lie sideways towards him. Were the

5 Sages Yao and Shun: Chinese Sage Myths

Fig. 5.27 Pottery vessels from the Qijia culture, Guanghe, Gansu

women die when the man died, or were they human sacrifice for the man? Either way, the superiority of men and the inferiority of women was obvious. Also, it proved that the difference in man and woman's status was not invented by Confucianism, as it existed 4,000 years ago in Northwest China.

Surrounding the Qijia joint burial were pottery pots. Qijia culture stemmed from a local kingdom around 4,000 years ago. The shapes of the potteries were identical, from Qinghai to South Ningxia and Longdong, Gansu. In 2004 in Guanghe, Gansu, where Qijia culture was named, the local government wanted to advocate the local culture, so they built a display room to showcase the objects from the antique warehouse. They ended up with a whole wall of displays. These were the intact pottery vessels left by people from 4,000 years ago (see Fig. 5.27). Those pots were fragile, but these many intact potteries were found in the warehouse of a town meant a large population and prosperity. That was surprising.

A single county had so many relics to display. With 2,800 counties in China, how many pieces of relics there could be 4,000 years ago? The Liuwan Museum in Qinghai had dozens of thousand pieces of colored potteries locked in the warehouse. Because of limited financial ability, the small museum in the village only displays five hundred selected objects. Most are still sealed in boxes.

The Chinese prehistoric culture is splendid and grand. Through a review of the era of Yao and Shun, we followed the Yellow River and examined areas from Central China to Hetao region and the Northwest region at the upper stream. This is a brand-new approach in research. Many of the issues I discussed are just the findings of my own research, and I hope they inspire some thinking in you.

Chapter 6
Gun and Yu Control the Waters: Chinese Flood Myths

Hang Qian

Professor Hang Qian holds a Ph.D. in history. He is a professor and doctoral supervisor in Department of History at the School of Humanities and Communications, Shanghai Normal University. He is also an adjunct professor and doctoral supervisor in Department of History at East China Normal University. Professor Qian serves as a member of the academic board and an adjunct researcher at Centre for Historical Anthropology at Sun Yat-sen University, which is a national key research base. He is also an executive director at China Society of Social History. His research interests are history of Chinese society, clan system history, historical anthropology, and historical geography.

Yu the Great 大禹 *da yu* is one of the most well-known figures in Chinese mythology. For thousands of years, the legends of Yu the Great were processed, shaped, passed on and had a tremendous impact on Chinese history. Why did the legends of Yu the Great come into being? Were they based on reality? What inspiration have the legends of Yu the Great left for modern humanity? In this lecture, I will introduce the latest research results on his legends from mythological, historical, geographical, anthropological, and hydraulic engineering aspects.

It is said that Gun 鲧 and Yu were father and son. The topic "Gun and Yu Control the Waters: Chinese Flood Myths" is an interesting one. Although the era they lived is distant from ours, we can still find traces of their stories in our life. Therefore, it is important to understand the images from the legends as we discuss our confidence in Chinese culture in the 21st century. I will discuss later why I am using the word "image" instead of "human". In the 1930s, Mr. Lu Xun, a famous Chinese writer, and Mr. Gu Jiegang, a historian of the Doubting History School, had a serious debate on whether Yu the Great was human or god; so serious that this debate led to personal resentment between the two. Now after decades, we bring back this discussion, but it is out of the respect for Chinese traditional culture.

Let's put aside Gun, and discuss Yu first. His name has several variations, including the Big Yu 大禹, Xia Yu 夏禹, and the Emperor Yu 帝禹. According to Sima Qian's *Records of the Grand Historian* 史记, Yu was the founder of the Xia dynasty; that is why he was called Xia Yu. Xia is a real dynasty in the Chinese history, but where was its capital? What specific texts and relics are left? Now historians and scholars have not reached a consensus. The archaeologists are also unclear about the location of Xia's capital and will need further research and concrete evidence. We can basically say that the Erlitou site in Henan belonged to the Xia dynasty, but it is hard to say that it was the capital. Nowadays with the growth of national power, the academic community has focused more attention to the Xia dynasty. I believe the research and development on this topic will continue, because the border has already been roughly defined. Yu was the founding emperor of the Xia dynasty, as referenced in Sima Qian's *Records of the Grand Historian*. "Big" 大 in "the Big Yu" 大禹 means "great" in Chinese. Many words in ancient China are commonly associated with greatness, such as 大 *da*, 太 *tai*, and 泰 *tai*. In ancient times, being named 大 and 太 was a great honor. That is true in modern Chinese as well.

Because of Yu's great achievements, later generations created various images in paintings and statues to commemorate him. People also turned the places he might have been to into memorial venues. As far as we know, people have been commemorating him since around four thousand years ago. By the time of the Spring and Autumn Period and the Warring States Period, there were large-scale commemorating structures. Today, we can still see some of those, such as King Yu's Mausoleum Temple 大禹陵 in Shaoxing, Zhejiang. It is quite close to us and it is very convenient to pay a visit. Yu the Great is one of the most famous figures in the legendary era of China. For thousands of years, the legends of Yu have been processed and shaped, leaving tremendous impact on Chinese history. Why did those legends come into being? Were the legends of Yu based on reality? What lessons do the legends of Yu teach us modern people? These three questions are what we seek to answer today. Some answers are the consensus of the academic community, and some are my personal opinions, which may not be necessarily right. Still I want to share my thoughts with you, from the perspective of mythology, history, geography, anthropology, and hydraulic engineering. It is impossible to figure out what actually happened, as most of the historical evidence has long been destroyed, but we can try to get closer to the answers. That is my guiding principle, which is to seek truth from facts.

We can find a lot of images of Yu the Great, but no one has seen him in person. In the past, Mr. Gu Jiegang held that Yu was a worm. While laughable, it actually made some sense. Later, people thought that since he was an emperor, he should look like an emperor. Therefore, many images of a mighty emperor appeared as the later generations used the great emperors of their times to shape prehistoric characters. For example, the hats in Fig. 6.1 only appeared after the Han Dynasty (see Fig. 6.1).

Quite a few parks are themed Yu the Great, but the best one is in Shaoxing, Zhejiang. So how do we picture Yu? Should we think of him more as the mighty emperor, or as the leader who curbed the flood? The image of the emperor that I just showed you is in fact inconsistent with his image in the *Records of the Grand Historian*. He was more like a common person than an emperor. With a tool in hand, he commanded a large team to work on the water control project. He might have the charisma of an emperor, but he was more like a charismatic organizer, a leader in controlling the flood (see Fig. 6.2).

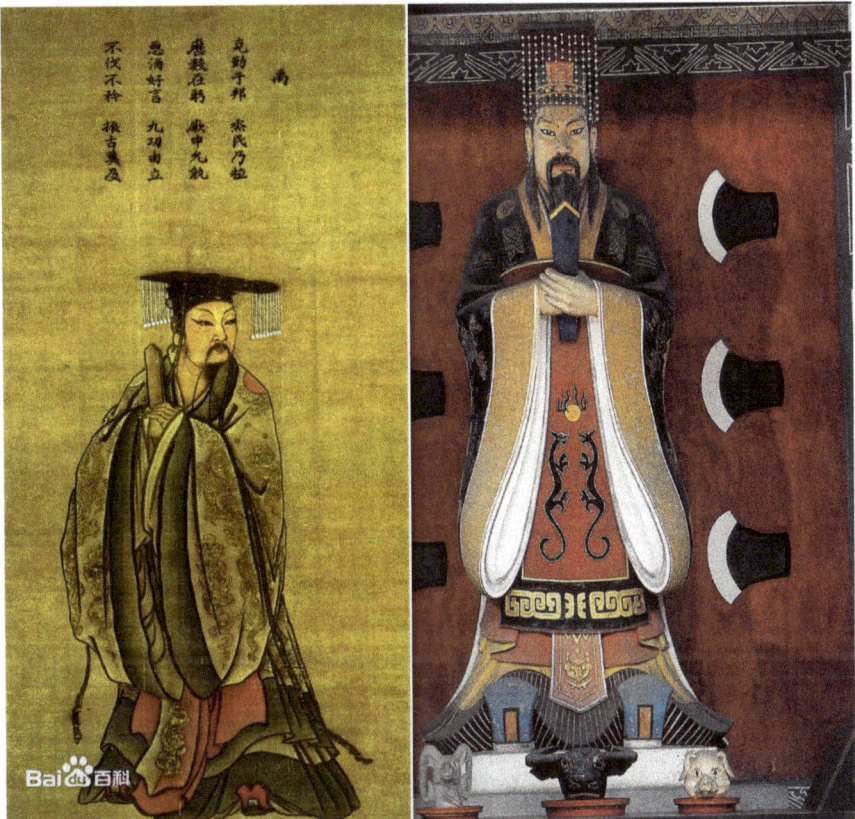

Fig. 6.1 Image of Yu the Great

The image of Yu has become the business card of Shaoxing, Zhejiang. This can be traced back to the Spring and Autumn Period. In *Spring and Autumn Annals of Wu and Yue* 吴越春秋, a historical record of the two southern states of Wu 吴 and Yue 越 during Spring and Autumn Period, we can tell that Yu had been a household name. We don't know how people in the era of Yu thought of him, but we do know how people in the Warring States Period viewed him, as proposed by Chinese historian Gu Jiegang. He said: "We have no way of knowing the history of the Xia, Shang and Zhou dynasties, but we can learn about how the people in the Spring and Autumn Period and the Warring States Period thought of the three dynasties." All those structures, according to the records of *Spring and Autumn Annals of Wu and Yue*, have already existed in the Spring and Autumn Period and the Warring States Period. Of course, those were no match to today's structures in terms of scale or craftsmanship, but they were probably built in the same places, indicating that the image of Yu had been consistent since the Spring and Autumn Period and the Warring States Period (see Fig. 6.3).

Fig. 6.2 Yu in the image of a common person

This kind of archway-style buildings appeared later, commonly believed to be in the Song and Yuan dynasties (see Fig. 6.4). The tomb of Yu was called 陵 *ling*. This particular word *ling* refers to emperors' tombs after the mid Warring States. But in earlier days, *ling* simply represented the land and mountains, without special reference to emperors. Yu's tomb was called *ling*, not by people of his era, but by people of later generations. Through the image of Yu, we can tell that people were more willing to regard him as a human, instead of a god. Gods in ancient Chinese myths should be able to fly, but Yu was always grounded and standing on the earth. In the Chinese mythology system, the gods of land and the gods of heaven belong to the same system. Under the ground, there are more ghosts, as we can tell from stories about the hell. Yu is not found in any of the systems. The ancient China has two major mythology systems, Kunlun and Penglai. In neither of the systems can you find the image of Yu. It means that the ancient people still wanted to regard Yu as a person, but he was not an ordinary person!

Fig. 6.3 Structures commemorating Yu the Great

After Yu arrived, he dug a well and was ready to settle down. He seemed to be very tired after living a hectic life, and wanted to find a place to call home, so he started digging the well. Gradually, this place developed into a town. This is a statue of Yu in Shaoxing (see Fig. 6.5). From the statue, we can tell that people's imagination of Yu stabilized. They did not think of Yu as an emperor, although it would be easily acknowledged.

Fig. 6.4 Archway-style structures

Fig. 6.5 Statues of Yu

If we talk about Yu as an emperor, no one will object. But as time goes by, people are more inclined to introduce Yu from the palace to the common daily life, and to consider him as a leader that common people can understand and approach, instead of an imposing emperor with a hat. While the image of Emperor Yu still exists, it is still the image of Yu the civilian that impresses and inspires us the most.

During a lecture in Xiaoshan, Zhejiang, I shared my thoughts about local commemorating activities. In the past, at Yu's Mausoleum in Shaoxing, local governments at all levels had been holding grand memorial activities every year, mainly at the provincial and municipal levels. Mayors and local governors all had to give formality speeches in royal yellow robes. I thought that it might be problematic to associate Yu with an emperor. I suggested that we should remember Yu as a common person, whom we could relate to and whose actions could be our examples. That might be his most important legacy. As a social influencer, we should grasp the direction of cultural guidance and use our judgment of value to understand an ancient figure.

Back to our topic, when we look at these images, we will certainly have this question: Is Yu a human or a god? To his people, was he a civilian, a leader or a lofty emperor? The emperor was the closest to god. He was not to easily reveal his emotions or actions. Was this image like Yu? Was it why people called him "great"? Some people may say that he is both a god and a man, which is a vague answer. What elements of a god and of a man he had, and at what percentage, this question often appears in our mind when we discuss ancient characters. For example, mythological characters Monkey King and Zhu Bajie also pose the same question. Another example is the myth of Chang'e flying to the moon. People tend to infer the behavior of Chang'e from the details that people can understand. Almost all myths are about how people understand deities and how to interpret their behaviors. As Marx said, God is the creation of man.

A deity in the image of a man 人形神迹, that is the usual answer. It can be a character in a myth: a deity, or a supernatural being, whose conducts are perfectly understandable to human beings. Yu the Great looks like a human, but does things that cannot be achieved by ordinary people, so we say he is a deity in the image of a man. That is the logic. When something beyond human capability is achieved, we call the creator a deity or close to a deity. In our daily life, we have similar metaphors. For example, when we see the wonders of nature, we say that it is created by ghosts' axes and deities' craftsmanship 鬼斧神工. Some people have photographic memory, and we say their memories connect to deities 通神. I have a friend with a remarkable memory. Given any place name, he can immediately respond with the unique sceneries, food, or language in that place. We think that it is remarkable ability, as we cannot find such information even with dictionaries in our hands. So we say that his memory connects to deities. For achievements that are beyond ordinary people, we always relate them to deities. For the same reason, Yu is called "the Great". When we talk about human nature, we talk about the joys and sorrows that people generally have. The image of Yu has human elements, but also transcends ordinary humanity. What Yu did is definitely what people would do, but is beyond what ordinary people can achieve.

Therefore, we cannot provide a simple verdict on whether Yu is human or a god. We cannot confirm if he is human or divine. Perhaps some people would think that such an answer is ambiguous, but this is what research on mythology and legends is. Any simple conclusion that "Yu is human" or "Yu is divine" is bound to be questioned from the following angles.

We say that Yu behaves like a deity in the image of human, because some historical evidence is found. We don't know how Yu wrote, but it is said that his handwriting was passed down (see Fig. 6.6). In theory, there was no writing in Yu's era, but thousands of years later, people claimed that Yu's handwriting was found—that fits our imagination that Yu is both divine and human. His handwriting is called Yu's Calligraphy 禹迹. Stone tablets engraved with his writing are called Tablets of Yu's Calligraphy 禹迹碑, which are found in several places in China. The picture shows Yu's calligraphy, originally from Hengshan, Hunan province. The characters are hardly recognizable, and we need to guess. No one today has ever met Yu the Great, and no one can say that they can recognize his writing, because we have no idea whether writing existed back then, and if yes, what the characters looked like.

This tablet is also known as God Yu Tablet 神禹碑 or Gou Lou Tablet 岣嵝碑, which is said to be engraved when Yu was managing the floods. It was originally on Zhurong Peak in Hengshan Mountain. Because the mountain is also called Gou Lou Mountain, this tablet is also called Gou Lou Tablet. There is also a tablet on Yuelu Mountain, which is said to have been copied and carved from Gou Lou Tablet by Zhi He 何致 of the Southern Song dynasty. Why did he do that? It was related to the overall environment. The Song dynasty was under a cultural crisis as it was being invaded by the northern minorities, so it paid special attention to restoring the tradition of Xia, Shang and Zhou dynasties. In fact, during the entire Song dynasty,

Fig. 6.6 Handwriting of Yu the Great

the government was dealing with wars with foreigners. In the Southern Song dynasty, to restore the traditional Chinese culture in the Central Plains, the government spared no effort in excavating, protecting, and promoting ancient legacies. In ancient China, whenever the traditional culture was promoted, it was either at the peak or the weakest moment of national strength. The Song dynasty was not the weakest or poorest in Chinese history, but it needed to boost its cultural confidence, so there was so much preservation effort. Along with that is many forgeries. It is well known that people in the Song dynasty were skilled in duplicating and false making. This is part of the textual research from the Southern Song dynasty on Yu's handwriting, which is now kept in the Palace Museum. The full text is lost in history.

The most important evidence to prove that Yu is a human being is the handwriting that we just mentioned. Others are all textual records, which mainly hold that Yu is divine and human. He speaks the language of ordinary people but does things that ordinary people are unable to achieve. From the beginning of the Zhou dynasty of three thousand years ago, people started recording Yu's deeds on various implements.

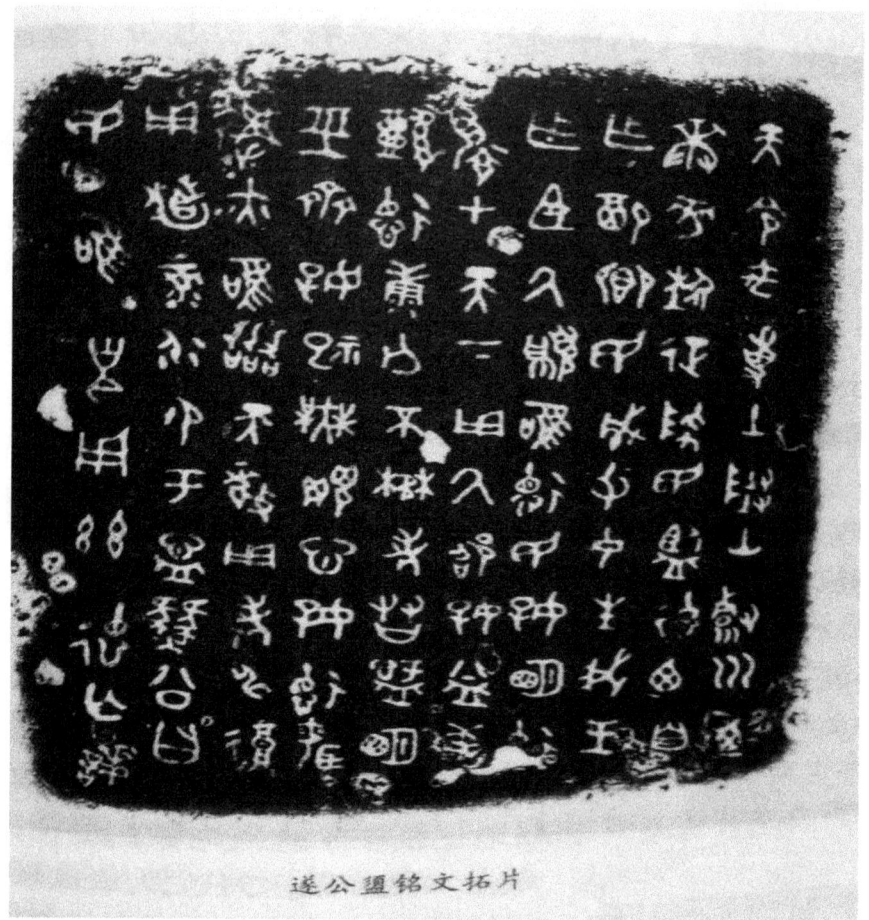

Fig. 6.7 Rubbing from the inscriptions on the Duke Sui Vessel

Most were found on ritual bronzes, because they could last for a long time. This is a piece of rubbing from the inscriptions on the Duke Sui Vessel 遂公盨 at the end of West Zhou dynasty, which mentions the story of Yu (see Fig. 6.7).

Mr. Xueqin Li believes that the inscriptions "天命禹敷土, 随(堕)山浚川" refers to the story of Yu controlling the water. It means that Yu was tasked by heaven to curb the flood, which he completed by flattening the mountains and dredging the rivers. Yu's contribution cannot go unnoticed and will pass down for generations. The discovery of this inscription moved Yu's story back by six to seven hundred years. Previously, the consensus was that only after the Spring and Autumn Period and the Warring States Period, the legends of Yu began to exist. However, with the discovery of the bronze ritual wares, we found a much earlier record and that is the earliest known and most detailed written record of Yu. It shows that Yu's merits were on people's lips as early as 2,900 years ago. Although Yu has done things that are beyond ordinary people's capability, he for sure had managed the flood. Mythology is not created in a vacuum, nor the product of pure fabrication of later generations. It is unlike the story of Chang'e flying to the Moon. We can't say that people in the Han dynasty had gone off to the moon. We can only say that there was a desire to fly in the sky, and then people created deities that could do it. This is what later generations imagined based on the wishes of the earlier generations. However, Yu's controlling the flood is not what the later generations imagined, but what actually happened. Why didn't people of his era record his deeds? Because there was no way to do so. There may have been other methods, but we don't know yet. What we have known is that the people of Zhou dynasty had recorded the story of Yu's controlling the flood. There is still a wide gap that needs other methods to make up.

"Long-lived and Prosperous" from *The Book of Songs* 诗经 长发 is an ode in honor of Emperor Tang and his predecessors of the Shang dynasty. The following verse has been quoted in all the research on Yu: "Profoundly wise were [the lords of] Shang, and long had there appeared the omens [of their dignity]. When the waters of the deluge spread vast abroad, Yu arranged and divided the regions of the land, and assigned to the exterior great States their boundaries, with their borders extending all over [the kingdom]. Then the State of Song began to be great, and God raised up the son [of its daughter], and founded [the Family of] Shang[1] 浚哲维商, 长发其祥。洪水芒芒, 禹敷下土方。外大国是疆, 幅陨既长。有娀方将, 帝立子生商." These lines put Yu's water control efforts against the background of the outbreak of the Great Flood. Thus, the change in the nature is connected to the great achievements of Yu. In "Annals of the Xia" in *Records of the Grand Historian* 史记夏本纪, Sima Qian systematically wrote the history of Xia based on legends of Yu, although he had not read any literature from the Yu's era. In "Annals of the Xia", Yu has a surname and a first name, and his father and grandfather could be traced. He is described as an ordinary person. His characteristics, personality, and the ins and outs of water management are all mentioned. In later times, people supplemented more materials based on their understanding, so that Yu's profiles and stories have been continuously completed. This is the history of man, one that shows the combination of an emperor and an ordinary person.

"Annals of the Xia" also mentioned that after Yu became the emperor, he "sat facing the south. He named his reigning dynasty Xiahou and surname Si 南面朝天下, 国号曰夏后, 姓姒氏." So he got his surname after he became the first emperor of the Xia dynasty. Why he has the name of 文命 wenming? Beside the saying that 文 is 纹 *wen (stripe)* and there had been many other explanations by later generations. They are not all reliable, however, for palm readers are normally good at far-fetching. They would claim that they had foreseen Yu is a great figure. *Records of the Grand Historian* tells the story of what Yu had done after he took the throne. What impressed us most in the accounts is that Yu was not a person who likes stability, but was an active person who liked to walk around and visit many places. He passed his throne to his son, which is what an ordinary emperor would do, and we could not see any

---

[1]Translation is found here: https://www.sacred-texts.com/cfu/sbe03/sbe03068.htm. Accessed on 11/9/2019.

god-like trait in that. This is also the history of scholars studying human and gods. It is an important part of myth creation. The historical background behind the mythology is critical to the understanding of the greatness of god and the limitations of human nature. In the face of the Great Flood, what Yu achieved is the core content of the Yu legend and the most important point for us to understand. "While the flood was surging, Yu managed the land and the four corners 洪水芒芒, 禹敷下土方. Fu 敷 can be interpreted as depart, scatter, land, standing point while 方 meant directions. Facing the flood, Yu's actions were related to land. "During Yao's reign, the world was not in peace. Flood swept over land without boundary 当尧之时, 天下犹未平。洪水横流,泛滥于天下" "During Shun's reign, Gonggong stirred up the flood, which loomed close to Kongsang 舜之時, 共工振滔洪水, 以薄空桑." According to *Zhuangzi: Autumn Floods* 庄子秋水篇, "during Yu's reign, nine years out of ten were flooded 禹之时, 十年九潦." Another record "during Yu's time, flood lasted for seven years 禹七年水" showed that flood was very serious around Yu's era.

While bronze is the longest-preserved carrier, the large collection of bamboo slips during the Warring States Period in the Shanghai Library is also very valuable. The bamboo slips were collected from Hong Kong previously, part of whose contents receive different views by academia. The picture below shows an excerpt from the article "Rong Cheng Shi 容成氏". The article is composed of 53 bamboo slips. They are the physical evidence to the deeds of ancient Chinese emperors from the Warring States period. Most contents on the 53 bamboo slips were about the deeds of Yu (see Fig. 6.8). The Chu bamboo slips of the Warring States show that the deeds of Yu was common knowledge. Of course, back then, knowledge was mainly circulated within the court, the aristocrats, and the high officials while how were they reserved among ordinary people remain unknown.

Through the bamboo slips *Rong Cheng Shi*, we know that Yu's stories have long been common knowledge in the middle and upper classes and are no secret. People just had not agreed on whether Yu was more like a deity or a human, but there was no question that he had existed.

It is very remarkable that *Rong Cheng Shi* can be preserved so well. Bamboo slip preservation is quite complex. People can restore the slips to a certain extent, but there is no guarantee that every restoration effort will be successful. The wellbeing of the slips shows that the preservation technology was very advanced at the time. Today, the writing on these bamboo slips is still very clear, and the ink formula is very particular. Researchers used to believe that the drier the environment, the longer the bamboo slips last. Later, the excavations of various tombs of the Spring and Autumn Period and the Warring States Period proved that moisture was also one of the important conditions for preserving ancient documents. It is said that a special chemical liquid was used. Although the formula and proportion of chemicals can be restored by modern scientists, the testing results are not ideal. Another example is that the very sharp arrow found near the terracotta warriors can still peel pears today. Test results show that electroplating technology was involved, and chromium came from the quenching of plant ash. We can reproduce such arrows in laboratory today, but how did people in Emperor Qin's era operate such technology? The weapons in the Qin era were very sharp and were close to mass-production. The preservation

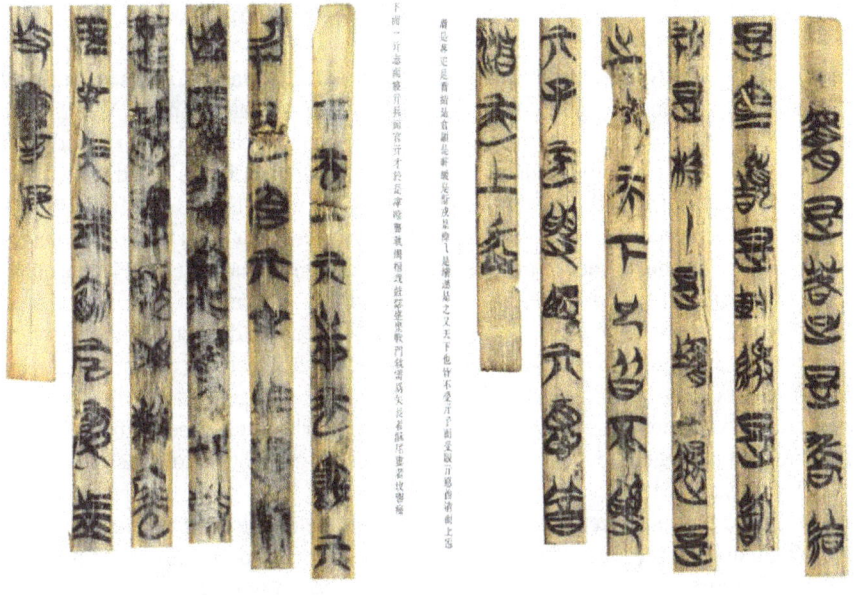

Fig. 6.8 Chu bamboo slips *Rong Cheng Shi* from the Warring States in the collection of Shanghai Museum (partial)

of these cultural relics of the Spring and Autumn Period attracts much attention in Chinese universities. Zhejiang University has done a good job as the school has experts on engineering physics, anthropology, and microbiology on board.

The stories told in *Rong Cheng Shi* all happened before the time of Sima Qian. We believe that there must be other documents of Yu's stories that we haven't found. The most important content in the article is Yu's control of water. While there were no details of his flood control, there were descriptions of the achievements. We long to know more about the details, but at that time, that document did not provide many; only the grand and general ideas were mentioned. Some of them were the main methods of engineering technology, such as excavation and blocking. Yu blocked the grand lake Mingdu, dug nine rivers, so that Yanzhou and Xuzhou could be inhabited; he dredged the Huaihe and Yishui rivers so that they can flow into the sea and made Qingzhou and Juzhou inhabitation; he dredged the Ouyi and Yishui rivers and let them flow into the sea, so that Bingzhou became inhabitable; he dredged three rivers and five lakes, and let them flow east into the sea, so that Jingzhou and Yangzhou could be inhabited; he dredged the Yi and Luo rivers, merged the two streams Chan and Jian, and let them flow east into the Yellow River, so that Yuzhou could be inhabited; he dredged Jing and Wei rivers, and let them flow north into the Yellow River, so Yongzhou became inhabitable. These became important clues for future generations to understand Yu's water control methods.

So Yu indeed controlled the floods. Why is the legend of Yu associated with water management? It's because of the phrase "洪水茫茫" in *The Book of Songs* 诗经 长发. We know that already. Later, some historians' claim that Yu was a worm is also related to water. Yu's greatness is related to his achievements in water control. What is the historical background of the legend of Yu? Whether there had been a Great Flood? Is it possible to recover with modern natural science? The answer is yes! Earth scientists' research proved that after the quaternary glaciation, between 13,000 and 10,500 years ago, the earth entered the post-glacial period. Between 7,000 and 6,500 years ago, the melting of ice sheets caused the sea level 2–4 m higher than today's. The process of sea level rising formed a "sea invasion" and the earth entered a "transgression period". Large areas, including Egypt, Babylon, Greece, and North America, were hit by floods. This can prove that at that time, the entire planet was under the deluge. Therefore, flooding is not a poet's literary creation, but a general affirmation of a distant history, which was not expressed through written characters, but through exaggerated language about people's memories from generation to generation. The great flood was a real episode in history.

During the Renaissance, the famous painter Michelangelo's "The Flood", based on biblical stories, preserved the memory of the Great Flood in the western world (see Fig. 6.9). Our recorded history of civilization spans only tens of thousands of years. The entire human history, according to anthropologists, can be traced back to six million years ago. Before the flood, human had millions of years of development but never experienced flooding. Therefore, panic was inevitable. According to the Bible, God ordered Noah to bring earth species to the ark to escape. This is the story of Noah's Ark where only one male and one female member of each species can be taken to flee. With this type of flood, the sea level rose 2–4 m. In comparison, with the current global warming, the melting of the Arctic ice sheet will only raise the sea level by one meter. The rise in sea level has led to changes in geophysical properties, tsunami, and earthquakes. So the descriptions in the Bible were true. God saw the Great Flood, found Noah, the good man, and taught him how to take refuge. Since then, the Noah family had been building the Ark for 120 years until the flood came. Noah's family of eight got on the ark, with a pair of animals from each species. They survived and multiplied. This is a story, though it can hardly be real, who can determine that it was made up? In the East Asian region where China is located, there have been five large-scale floods between 10,000 years ago and 4,000 years ago, which were proved by archaeologists and geophysicists. The last occurrence was approximately 4,700 to 4000 years ago, during the era of Yao, Shun, and Yu. The evidence is that at a certain level of a mountain, we discovered something that came from the sea, so we know that the place used to be below the sea level.

The floods ended around 4,200 to 4,000 years ago, which happened to be in the era of Yu (see Fig. 6.10). The officially determined chronology of Xia started around four thousand years ago which means that from the perspective of modern earth sciences, we can also confirm that there had been a major flood in Yu's era.

There is no Noah's Ark in Chinese mythology, but what do we have? Let us look at the character 船 (ship). What can we imagine? Aren't there eight mouths (八、口) on the side of the ship (舟)? This is a research method in history study. The

Fig. 6.9 Scenes from "The Flood"

famous politician and diplomat Zhang Zhidong of the late Qing dynasty had discussed how to study Chinese traditional culture by studying the Chinese characters: If one learned characters before studying Chinese Classics, his Classics Studies will be solid; from there, if he goes on into History, then his History Studies will be solid 由小学入经学者, 其经学可信; 由经学入史学者, 其史学可信. Study in primary school is to learn, to recognize, and to explain the meanings of characters. Classics are the principles and norms. I often tell my students that we must learn to analyze Chinese characters, which can inspire associations. Based on the mere character 船, we cannot say that China also has a Noah's Ark legend. But can we, in turn, say the story about Noah's family of eight on the Ark is purely fictional? We don't dare to make specific conclusions, but this is a very interesting coincidence. A boat, a boat with

B.C.	The Xia dynasty	
2070	Yu 禹	
	Qi 启	Son of Yu
	Tai Kang 太康	Son of Qi
	Zhong Kang 仲康	Younger brother of Tai Kang
		Son of Zhong Kang
	Xiang 相	
	Shao Kang 少康	Son of Xiang
	Yu 予	Son of Shao Kang
	Huai 槐	Son of Yu
	Mang 芒	Son of Huai
	Xie 泄	Son of Mang
	Bu Jiang 不降	Son of Xie
	Jiong 扃	Younger brother of Bu Jiang
	Jin 廑	Son of Jiong
	Kong Jia 孔甲	Son of Bu Jiang
	Gao 皋	Son of Kong Jia
1600	Fa 发	Son of Gao
	Gui (Jie) 癸(桀)	Son of Fa (some believe he is the younger brother of Fa)

Fig. 6.10 Xia's chronology

some people, and some animals that can reproduce: these are imaginable. The most important lesson is that in the face of the flood, one cannot escape alone. Nowadays, many American movies have themed about deserted islands. People trapped there must cooperate and multiply. I cannot but wonder, what would Yu and his ancestors do with the flood?

Thus, there go into a hypothesis of the ancient history, that is, Yu the Great, like Yellow Emperor, Emperor Yan, Shao Hao, Gonggong, Yao, and Shun, are all famous ancient "legend period" characters. In recent years, they are all generally identified by researchers in modern times as the chiefs of tribal groups in the late period of the primitive society. In other words, they are not necessarily individuals, but maybe the clan leaders who inherited the same names. When a leader named the Yellow Emperor passed away, the successive leaders also inherited this name. That is the reason why the legends of the Yellow Emperor had spaned hundreds and thousands of years, which is not possible with a single person. The same is true for Yu the Great, all the people we saw in the legends above were of hundreds of years old. Scholars from the Song Dynasty have tried to calculate how an ancient legendary character could live for five hundred or even seven hundred years. How to explain reasonably? Thus they worked out a whole set of calculations. Ouyang Xiu (a famous poet in the Song dynasty), for example, was fond of implementing such calculation. In fact, no calculation is needed. If the legend extends for seven hundred years, it simply means during the seven hundred years, the leaders had been called the same name. In this way, Yu the Great was over one hundred years old. Many names in the legendary era often served dual meanings: names of individuals and tribal groups. Some legendary figures lived far beyond the lifespan of humans. Only when their names are considered clan symbols do they seem closer to reality. Therefore, the Yellow Emperor, Emperor Yan, Shao Hao, Gonggong, Yao, Shun, and Yu can not only be understood as individuals but should be regarded as tribal groups led by these people or their successors.

The center of Xia dynasty's reign was in the western part of Anhui, Henan, and Shanxi on the Central Plains (see Fig. 6.11), mainly in the central part of China. However, the center of the reign does not equal to the scope of activities. The footprints of the Xia people spread throughout the land of China. The areas affected by sea transgression were mainly the outflow river basin and the southeast coast, which matched the area where Yu controlled. It does not matter whether Yu had actually been to those places. Legends had it that Yu's controlling water covered nine provinces and three rivers which were the major outflow rivers. In generations of storytelling, famous figures of ancient times and their tribal groups would come to be associated with the southeast coastal areas of Zhejiang at certain times.

Among them, Yu caught the most attention. It is possible that Yu reached the southeast coast of China. In the Taihu Lake Basin and the coastal areas of Jiangsu and Zhejiang, there are Poyang Lake and Sanjiang River. "Flow along with the river and the sea, reaching out to Huai River and Si River 沿于江海,达于淮、泗", "From the east most ocean to the west most deserts, from the north to the south, the emperor's virtue covers four seas (all directions) 东渐于海, 西被于流沙, 朔、南暨, 声教讫于四海." Again, this is the entire tribal group represented by Yu, who walked

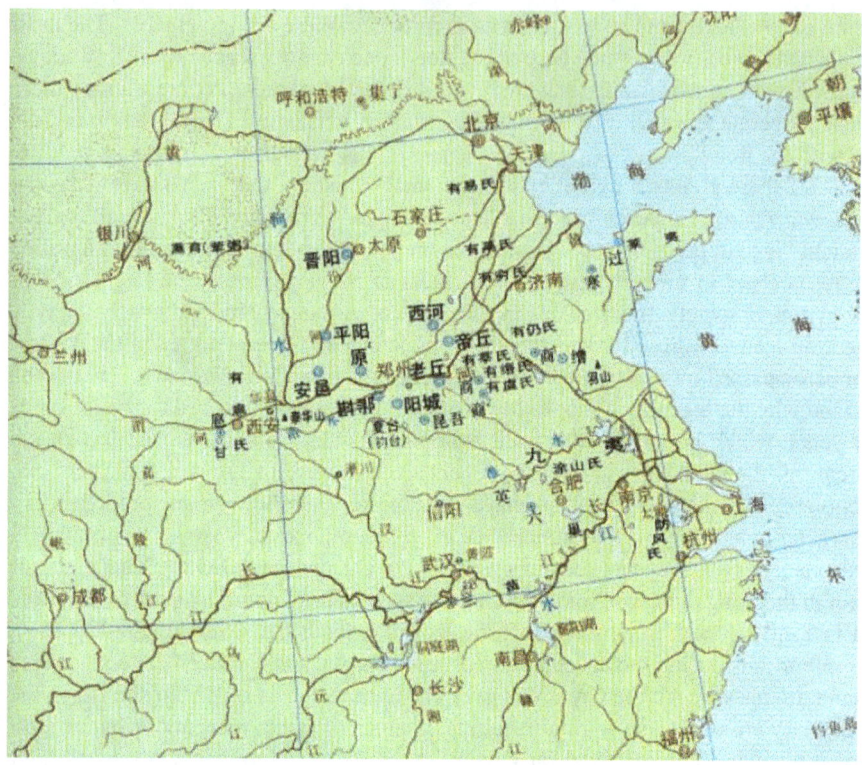

Fig. 6.11 Map of the Xia dynasty

along the water and managed the flood. Where the rivers flow, their footprints would follow. During the Three Kingdoms period, Wei Zhao from Danyang (in Jiangsu Province) said that Yu had been to Puyangjiang River. In the Southern Song dynasty, *Jiatai Chorography* 嘉泰会稽志 *Jiatai Kuaiji* Zhi quoted the *Old Classics* 旧经 that "Yu dredged the Liao River, so could people settle 禹疏了溪, 人方宅土." Those are the left traces of legends in texts. It is not necessarily accurate for ancient scholars to strictly interpret "Sanjiang" 三江 as within the areas of Wu and Yue. However, it is possible that Yu and his descendants and their tribal groups had been to Ningbo and Shaoxing areas in Zhejiang in order to control flood or to seek refuge. Later text as the Yue Jue Shu 越绝书 in the Warring States Period goes that "the people of the coastal areas of Yue used a special farming method, birds help with farming… answered: this practice was taught by Yu 大越海滨之民, 独以鸟田…曰:禹始也." "*niaotian* 鸟田" equals to "*xianggeng* 象耕", *tian* 田 is sounded as *dian* 佃, the same meaning as *geng* 耕, the verb farming. As Lunheng 论衡 by Wang Chong (27- c. 100 CE) goes: elephants and birds do the farming for people 象之为耕……鸟之为田.

During the transgression period, many Asian continents sank under the sea level, and the Ningshao Plain along the southeast coast of China became shallow sea. Modern technology can be used to find out the sedimentary history in this area, to see if it used to be the sea and how deep it was. The entire Shanghai area can also be surveyed like this. Therefore, I speculate that if Yu's water control was to be successful, it could not have been carried out during the peak period of the flood (transgression period), but only during the period of flood subsidence, that is, the sea withdrawal period. Between the transgression and regression of the sea, it could last as long as a few hundred years, or as short as several decades. Therefore, Yu possibly lived during the early stage of marine regression, when the land was slowly emerging. After the regression, there were lands, rivers, lakes, swamps and mountains in the coastal areas of Zhejiang, where human beings had the opportunity to survive with space for activities. Yu's Calligraphy that can be found all over the Ningshao Plain is to commemorate the positive actions of Yu, Yu's descendants and their tribal groups in this context. Although there is no specific scientific proof, we can see from the literature that Yu taught farmers to plant crops and adjust the salinity in the marshes, which were in line with the historical background at the time.

"Annals of the Xia" from *Records of the Grand Historian* records some important contents: "When traveling on land he used a carriage, on the water he used a boat, through miry he drove a sled, and when going over the hills he used spikes. In one hand he held the marking-line, and in the other the compass and square. Working as the seasons permitted, he held a view to open up the nine continents, nine roads, banking up nine marshes and to survey nine hills. He assigned his servant Yi to teach citizens that paddy should be planted in low damp places and directed Hou Ji to supplement citizens when they were difficult to obtain food. When food was scarce, he bartered the dukes' surplus stock in exchange for what they had not, so as to put all the states on an equal footing. Yu in this way worked for the mutual convenience of the respective districts as regards the distribution of the wealth and resources of the country 陆行乘车，水行乘船，泥行乘橇，山行乘檋。左准绳，右规矩，载四时，以开九州，通九道，陂九泽，度九山。令益予众庶稻，可种卑湿。命后稷予众庶难得之食。食少，调有余相给，以均诸侯。禹乃行相地所有以贡，及山川之便利。" All the natural scenes had appeared. During the period of the Flood, one can only do is to refuge. The basic principle of Yu was to adapt to local conditions. Therefore, I feel that our understanding of Yu should be put into the context of marine transgression and regression (see Fig. 6.12).

The Chinese were actively governing, while the Westerners were passively fleeing. But is this really the case? Is the history of Western governance of nature short? Here, I have speculation: to defend against the Great Flood, the ancestors before Yu were constantly building dams, which was actually not worth the time. At that moment, people should first escape and retreat by moving up to the highlands. Many Neolithic sites can be seen along the southeast coast, which were all inundated during the Great Flood. Did the residents at the time just sit there and wait to die? Absolutely not. If we understand a little about ancient mythology, we can imagine that they probably saw the sea rise and retreated into the forest. The choices of human beings follow such a path: from the coastal to the Central Plains, to the interior, and to the mountains. This had been the paths of human beings for 10,000 years, which might be related to the history of the Great Flood. Therefore, residents of different places, such as the mountain people, peasants, or citizens, are the result of historical formation and do

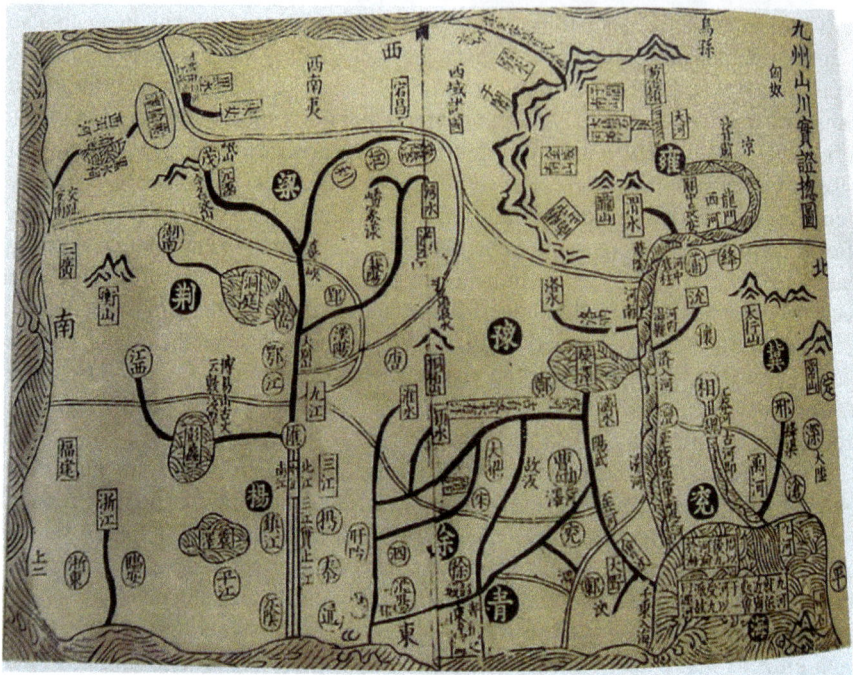

Fig. 6.12 Mountains and Rivers map in Jiuzhou (Nine regions)

not necessarily reflect their own willingness. Many minority groups have had such migration in history and been slowly driven to the places where they live today by some more powerful ethnic groups. This is the need for survival, not the embodiment of individual will. This reflects the perspective of anthropology.

After the sea regressed, various methods were wanted for survival. Yu taught people an important survival skill, planting rice in low-lying wetlands. Although we cannot say that it was " water rice" like nowadays, it was at least not the "land rice" of the Neolithic period. The specific planting details have certainly gone missing, but the fact of "planting" rice was registered. This is also the imagination and creation associated with Yu's legends.

In my opinion, Yu's marriage to his wife who was the daughter of Tushan, also took place during his retreat. His wife was from Tushan. But mountains named Tushan can be found everywhere in China, including Henan, Anhui, Sichuan, Zhejiang and many other cities. Today, Xiaoshan Jinhua Town also has Tushan, 335.8 m above sea level with steep mountain slope that was easy to flood. People moved into the mountains may because of refuge. People living in the area around Ningshao Plain are deeply grateful to Yu. There is the following record in the *Records of the Grand Historian*: "The Emperor went hunting in Kuaiji and died. 帝禹东巡狩，至于会稽而崩." Hunting referred to the ancient emperors inspecting their territories, but it could also mean that they were retreating. It was very wise to evacuate and

Fig. 6.13 Bianshi stone from when Yu was buried

retreat. Kuaiji does not necessarily refer to Shaoxing. In fact, Shun and Yu were not necessarily particular individuals who existed. It is quite reasonable for any capable person in charge of flood control to retreat to Kuaiji and managed water there. As long as the deeds were the same or slightly similar, no matter who they were, they could become respected gods in the eyes of the later generations, let alone Yu the Great. A pavilion in Shaoxing associated with the death of Yu was called the Bianshi Pavilion 窆石亭. This stone is said to be the stone from the Yu's era. After Yu was buried here, this stone was placed on the top (see Fig. 6.13). People in ancient China especially liked to use stones from pagodas to commemorate great men, which is said to be related to phallic worship.

The stories of Yu's visits to the mountain forest in ancient times were all related to the legends of the Great Flood, from which we can be inspired with the following points.

The first is to accurately analyze the water conditions rather than to take reckless actions. Yu's success is rooted in his relatively accurate understanding of the flood. Water and fire are merciless and do not tolerate hesitation. When the time comes, one should be ready to leave without any belongings. "As long as green hills remain, there'll never be a shortage of firewood." Therefore, when facing floods, to protect people's lives is the most important thing. Because the flood disaster was fierce and sudden, if someone could roughly understand the water situation, lead people to take refuge in time, and reduce the loss of life, he would certainly be respected. Such a leader and his clan would gradually turn into legends as people kept telling their stories. Yu was one of the most important representatives. In ancient legend, his accomplishments included managing water, soil, and crops. Other stories relating to Yu, such as "defeating *youmiao* group", "uniting dukes" and "debuting nine regions", are relatively rooted in flood-controlling and rice-farming legends. Earned time and saved lives, are the most important.

Second, choose the right solution. After lives were protected, people also had to figure out a plan. The ancient legend highly praised the water control technology of Yu, and compared his performance with that of Gonggong and his father Gun, who were responsible for water control, highlighting his wise choice: In the past, Gonggong tried to block rivers, flatten high grounds, and fill low-lying land, which harmed people under heaven. Heaven did not bless him, and people did not help him. With surging riots, Gonggong failed and was killed. In Youyu, there was a person named Gun, also known as Chongbo. He repeated Gonggong's mistakes, and was killed by Yao at the Yu Mountain. Later, Yu learned lessons from the past, and changed his strategy. He fortified the river banks, dug deeper the riverbed, dredged rivers so that no still water was left 昔共工……欲壅防百川, 堕高堙卑, 以害天下。皇天弗福, 庶民弗助, 祸乱并兴, 共工用灭。其在有虞, 有崇伯鲧, 播其淫心, 称遂共工之过, 尧用殛之于羽山。其后伯禹念前之非度, 釐改制量,……高高下下, 疏川导滞. It seemed that neither Gonggong's nor Gun's "defense" projects had been successful. Only Yu was able to learn from their failures. He changed "defense" into "dredging," and finally succeeded. In fact, water control technologies that various tribes adopted could not differ that much. Facing floods, the main strategy must have been building dams, with dredging as a supplementary method. As far as technology itself is concerned, as long as it was adapted to local conditions and guided by topography and water conditions, the use of one method or multiple methods could be effective. When the later generations built the reservoir, they used the "defense" damming method. Therefore, according to *Zuo Zhuan* 左传, in the seventeenth year of Zhaogong, *Tanzi* said that "the Gonggong clan's totem is related to water, so they control water and are named after water 共工氏以水纪, 故为水师而水名"; *Book of Rites, Sacrifice Law* 礼记祭法 also said that "Gonggong's clan was in charge of the nine continents. Gonggong's son named Houtu was able to settle the nine continents 共工氏之霸九州也, 其子曰后土, 能平九州." These all confirmed that Gonggong and his tribal group had made achievements comparable to Yu. If the natural laws of the sea regression were violated, all efforts would be in vain even if Yu came to rescue. *Huainanzi·Master Training* 淮南子·主术训 said: "Yu's water control benefited the world, but he was not able to make the rivers flow backward 禹决江疏河, 以为天下兴利, 而不能使水西流." We don't need to pay too much attention to Yu's specific methods in controlling water, because they cannot be verified. The success of Yu lies in sea regression, which provided the natural condition for the "dredging" method to be effective; Gun failed, because he went against the water. When water was making advances, it was impossible to achieve success in building dams. One can put in all the time and effort they want, but such investment does not guarantee success. Even now, with very advanced technology, it is not easy to protect the Yangtze River with dams!

Third, social status and divinity stem from morality. The reason that Yu is known as Yu the Great, is a result of his characters and merits. He passed by his home three times during his flood-control efforts, but he did not even enter once. He also persevered throughout the years, like the old man Yugong who finally removed a mountain. By the way, it is said that Yu and Yugong were connected in some way, but here we will not go down that rabbit hole. The completion of Yu's flood control project in thirteen years makes us believe that the scale of his project was limited based on the engineering conditions of the time. If he were to build dams, thirty years would not be enough!

In short, Yu the Great and his legends have left us with very rich historical contents, which are still being enriched and provide us food for thought. Although more than one hero must have made achievements comparable to Yu in 3,000 years of recorded history and beyond, there was only Yu the Great, who is still remembered and commemorated at such a large scale. Today, we can live a peaceful life on our land, part of the reason is attributed to Yu, as well as the concerted efforts of our whole nation represented by Yu. We commemorate him now, and we will continue to do so in the future!

Correction to: Myths of the Creation of Chinese

Correction to:
Z. Tian et al., *Myths of the Creation of Chinese*,
https://doi.org/10.1007/978-981-15-5928-0

The original version of the book was inadvertently published with a few errors. The book has also been updated with these corrections.

1. Change of author's affiliation for Shuxian Ye, changed "Zhiyuan College" to "Center for Study of Literary Anthropology".
2. The textual corrections have been carried out throughout the book.

The updated version of the book can be found at
https://doi.org/10.1007/978-981-15-5928-0

GPSR Compliance

The European Union's (EU) General Product Safety Regulation (GPSR) is a set of rules that requires consumer products to be safe and our obligations to ensure this.

If you have any concerns about our products, you can contact us on

ProductSafety@springernature.com

In case Publisher is established outside the EU, the EU authorized representative is:

Springer Nature Customer Service Center GmbH
Europaplatz 3
69115 Heidelberg, Germany

www.ingramcontent.com/pod-product-compliance
Lightning Source LLC
LaVergne TN
LVHW050013270326
834688LV00068B/38